The Spirit of Your Marriage

The Spirit of Your Marriage

How Christian couples can create a richer and more fulfilling marriage

DAVID J. LUDWIG

AUGSBURG Publishing House • Minneapolis

THE SPIRIT OF YOUR MARRIAGE

*This book is dedicated to
Kathy who has kept the
spirit of our marriage
very much alive by her
openness and loving confrontation*

Contents

Preface

THIS BOOK IS INTENDED for all persons who are married or who plan to become married. Its content grows out of extensive counseling with couples experiencing marital difficulties, yet it is not written primarily for those whose marriages are in trouble. Rather, this book is written with the hope of reaching your marriage before things get to the point where you need the help of a counselor. It is written primarily for preventive purposes to give you direction for working on your marriage.

You do need to work on your marriage because you live in a culture that is very hard on the marriage relationship. The things that would hold the two of you together in previous generations (such as community and family pressures) are disappearing. Marriages are vulnerable today! No union can be taken for granted and all marriages, including your own, need daily attention.

The focus of the book is upon the *spirit* of the marriage. Each relationship is a unique creation by God's Spirit. Your relationship is alive as long as its spirit is present. The use of the term, *spirit,* is not intended to introduce some nebulous concept or pious God-talk. Rather, it is an attempt to put some teeth into an all-important aspect of any relationship.

I came upon this concept through my counseling. I could see that something was missing between two people when they came in for help. In the cases where the marriage was restored, this something was again present in the relationship. The way they looked at each other and the way they talked to each other had changed. The spirit of their marriage had come back!

I write this book with the hope that you will be able to gain a better understanding of the spirit of your marriage. Perhaps your union can be strengthened by following the suggestions for working on your marriage. Any effort spent on your relationship will be worth it!

The use of case illustrations is intended to give you concrete examples to apply in your own situation. The cases are real, but changed sufficiently so that the individuals involved cannot be identified. The cases were chosen to illustrate typical ways in which the spirit of a marriage is killed and how it can be restored to life again.

I also write this book in awe of the potential of the marriage relationship. The relationship itself remains a mystery to me, but its importance in a person's life is hard to overestimate. The blessings of a good marriage are enough to have you pause to give thanks daily to God for the presence of the spirit in your marriage.

1 The Spirit of a Relationship

THE DAY SEEMED TO GO BY SO SLOWLY for Jeannie. She couldn't get her mind off of the celebration they had planned for their first week's anniversary. She was so much in love with Bob. She could picture him taking her into his arms and swinging her around. She felt warm all over with the thought as she prepared a special dinner for just the two of them.

Bob looked again at Jeannie's picture in front of him. It was about time to go home and he felt a sense of excitement. He felt so close to her. He had some work to do yet, but he paused for a moment to think of the first week of their marriage. She was quite a person! "Oh, hang the work," Bob thought to himself, "I'll come in early and finish it tomorrow."

The doorbell rang and Jeannie wondered who it might be. Her face lit up with excitement and surprise when she opened the door. Their eyes met with a burst of emotion, then Bob took Jeannie in his arms for an electrifying hug. Neither wanted to let go.

They walked into the house holding hands, playfully

bumping each other. When Bob blocked the doorway to the kitchen, Jeannie started tickling him and they ended up in another hug. Bob was full of questions and teasing comments as they prepared the supper. "Why didn't you have supper on the table when I got home?" Bob asked, playfully. With that, Jeannie took her wet hands and flicked water into his face. "Hey, quit that," Bob said as he grabbed her arms. They wrestled for a moment in a mock struggle, then ended up laughing as Jeannie pushed him out of the kitchen.

The anniversary meal lasted a long time. Bob was full of compliments about the food and they discussed many things. "What was your day like?" Jeannie wanted to know. "Bill was on my back again," Bob began and then proceeded to open up about his frustration with his boss. Jeannie wanted to know more about how this affected her husband. He talked about one encounter: "I was rushing to get the order out when Bill came up complaining . . ." As he went on, he knew that Jeannie understood and felt so close to her. He squeezed her hand in appreciation. He stopped talking and they just sat and looked at each other for a tender moment.

It was getting late when they did the dishes together. Bob was in a playful mood again and started bothering Jeannie. With mock seriousness she warned him to stop it. "And what will you do if I don't?" Bob challenged.

"This," Jeannie teased as she grabbed his arms and pinned him up against the wall. They laughed and looked at each other. Bob drew Jeannie close and kissed her. The dishes were forgotten . . .

Jim felt very heavy. His job had been very frustrating and he had so much to do yet before he went home. "Home," he thought to himself and a flash of pain crossed his face. He remembered how Sally had blown up at him that morning when he said he might have to work late. He shuddered to himself as he felt the anger in her voice. Remembering her face, cold and harsh, he let out a heavy sigh. There was so much pressure. Couldn't she understand that he had things that had to be done? He went back to work with a dull coldness in his stomach.

Sally felt like screaming when Jim slammed the door in her face. Here it was their tenth anniversary and all he could think of was working late. "He has no time for me anymore," she thought as her anger turned into tears. She felt miserable and unhappy as she lay on the couch sobbing for a long time. She felt ugly as she remembered how she screamed at Jim. Why did she act like that? "If only he would pay attention to me," she dreamed as she continued to feel that heavy sadness.

Jim felt trapped. It was time to go home, but there was still so much to be done. He started to put things away, but then saw something he really needed to get done. But as he began the work, he realized that it could wait another day. Still, it seemed more pleasant and peaceful to stay at work than to go home. In fact, in a moment of honesty, he thought to himself, "I really don't want to go home." Home just meant tension and more pain.

Sally did a lot of thinking during the day. She knew that she was driving Jim away by the way she landed into him. She wanted so much to start over, so she started thinking of how she might make the evening pleasant for both of them. A tiny bit of hope started to emerge as she fixed a special supper for just the two of them. She would feed the children early and they would eat after the kids were in bed. By the time Jim was due home, Sally was in a pretty good mood.

Sally waited for the sound of the car in the driveway

as she finished feeding the children. A half hour went by and she felt a dull pressure starting to form in her chest. "He really doesn't care about me," a voice said inside her, and she felt her good mood slipping. Another half hour went by and Sally started feeling foolish about having such high hopes. She wished she had not done so much preparing for their evening together. That angry feeling reappeared and was growing by the minute.

Jim knew he was going to catch it, so he braced himself as he walked in the door. There was icy silence as he hung up his coat and went to change clothes. Sally broke the silence, "Well, you could at least say goodnight to the children before they go to bed." Jim picked up the coldness in her voice and in silence walked past her to take the kids to their bedroom.

He enjoyed the children and spent a lot of time kidding and playing with them before they finally said their prayers. He felt comfortable with them and forgot about Sally for the moment. But then, as he came back into the living room, the tension hit again. "Hey, what's for supper?" he tried.

"Well, I had planned something very special for us, but you didn't seem to care." There was an edge in Sally's voice that made Jim wince. He sighed and went over to pick up the paper.

Then Sally blew up! "Can't you give me one minute of your time? You can't tell me that you have that much to do at work. Why were you late tonight?" As she cut into him, Jim felt the coldness grow in him until he was numb. He didn't look up, but kept his eyes on the paper with his teeth grinding away. "Here it goes again," he thought. He wished he were somewhere else.

Sally was hurt by his lack of response and felt like screaming at him. She caught herself and was smoldering as she went back to preparing their meal. She took the candles off the table and, with hopes completely dashed, she said flatly, "You can come eat now." Jim obeyed methodically and they ate in silence, never once looking at each other. The food slipped tastelessly down and the meal remained only half eaten. Sally was softly sobbing to herself as she washed the dishes, feeling lonely and unloved.

And so we have two couples, both eating their anniversay dinners at home. But what a difference! There was a good spirit between Bob and Jeannie. They were happy and excited about each other.

Jim and Sally were a different story. There was clearly something missing in their relationship. It doesn't take an expert to tell that! But what was it that was missing? What was causing all the tension and bad feelings? What had happened to their marriage? Where had the spirit gone?

First take a look at the word *spirit*. This is a word that has been ignored in our scientific age. It describes something intangible, something that can't be seen, heard, touched, smelled, or tasted. It is also something that cannot be controlled or manipulated. Modern technology deals with the objective—with tangible things that can be controlled. Apparently our culture had to put this word aside in its struggle to produce what it considers to be the good life.

But that doesn't mean that *spirit* does not exist! In fact, when the spirit is missing, everyone is painfully aware of its absence. So, what is this term trying to describe?

Take a look at how we use this term in talking about people. You can be in "good spirits." This means you feel a sense of worth or accomplishment and have a lot of energy. You feel on top of things and excited about what you are doing. You're feeling good and everyone knows it. You want to be around others and are interested in what's happening.

But a person's spirit can be broken. You know how you break a horse's spirit, don't you? You put pressure on the "free spirited" animal. A saddle, bridle, and then spurs keep the horse under control. Finally, the horse submits to the pressure and follows the rider's will. The horse is no longer free. Its spirit has been broken.

In the same manner, a person's spirit can be crushed. Too much pressure over a period of time will take its toll. I know a pastor whose spirit was broken:

> Greg took the call to a small-town parish with a lot of enthusiasm. He had a lot of ideas he wanted to try out. When he woke up in the morning, he was ready to go. In meetings, he was full of ideas. He visited all the members within the first 6 months. His preaching was so full of energy. But then a controversy arose. Greg tried to work for a peaceful solution, but found his words being twisted. For several years, he struggled to minister, but found his actions criticized at every turn. He felt suspicion when he spoke out in meetings. Faces would be unreceptive to his preaching and gradually his enthusiasm for that congregation dried up. Preaching became a struggle and there were always excuses not to visit the members. He would wake up feeling heavy and not feeling like going to the office that day. Everything he did then seemed to take so much effort. His spirit was broken!

We read in the Bible that God comforts such a "broken spirit" by his Holy Spirit. When we feel a sense of worthlessness, he reminds us that we are his children and that he cares for us. God takes the pressure off. He gives peace.

A closer look at the concept of spirit in Scripture suggests that the term is related to freedom and boldness or energy—it suggests being alive. The root meaning of both the Hebrew and Greek terms for spirit is "movement of air" or "breath." Thus the spirit, like the wind, is free to move where it wills (John 3:8). God creates this spirit in us (Gen. 1:2, Job 27:3, Isa. 42:5, and Zech. 12:1) and preserves it through his steadfast love (Job 10:12)—by continually renewing his relationship with us through forgiveness (Rom. 6). With the power of God's Spirit, we can take a deep breath, hold our head up and speak with boldness, no matter what we have done or what mess we have made of our lives. Through forgiveness, we are alive to God in Christ Jesus (Rom. 6:11).

So God's Spirit dwells in us (Rom. 8:6-17) and inspires (Num. 11:17-29), gives energy (Judg. 3:10), and infuses value and direction on a person's life (1 Cor. 2:5). All through the book of Acts, the Spirit is equated with boldness and directness—with energy. Peter, filled with the Holy Spirit, has the boldness to stand up to the powerful high-priestly family (Acts 4:8, 13). Stephen's boldness carries even to death (Acts 6, 7). This boldness is translated into direct confrontation in Acts 13:9, "But Paul, filled with the Holy Spirit, *looked intently at him* and said 'You son of the devil . . . ' "

In other words, the human spirit, like God's Spirit has something to do with energy. A person's spirit gives energy to confront life. However, when put under too much pressure over a length of time, the human spirit can be dampened. Pressure comes when a relationship starts breaking down. Guilt and a feeling of "have to" put the pressure on at this time.

When a relationship between two persons is good, each feels free to do things for each other—they want to be involved helping each other. "Want to" means there is no pressure, but a good spirit is at work. When, however, the relationship starts breaking down and the desire to do things for each other is no longer there, then pressure takes over. The people put demands on each other and the feeling of "have to" takes over. Over a longer period of time, such demands and pressure dampen a person's spirit.

Consider a child in two contrasting situations:

1. It was Saturday. Tommy was feeling good and wanted to surprise his mother. She had let him go to a movie the day before, so he quietly closed the door and proceeded to clean up his room. He was excited as he finished putting the final touches on his bed, thinking of his mother's surprise when she found his room clean.

2. Tommy had let his room go for most of the week. His mother had reminded him to clean things up again and again. So Saturday morning she woke him up with a threatening "You'd better clean this junk heap up before I take the belt out." Tommy winced and pulled the covers over his head as she left. Ten minutes later, he felt his body jerked out of bed with an angry—"Get with it" by his father. He stiffened, but sullenly and halfheartedly, he started picking up things.

In which of the two situations was there pressure? If the second situation occurred regularly over a period of time, Tommy will feel guilty and under pressure in his relationship with his parents. He won't have much spirit for doing things around the house.

So Tommy feels guilt and pressure when criticism, demands, and rebellion are part of the relationship and is in good spirits when there is love and close feelings. The key is in the word *relationship.*

Now, once again, God comforts a broken spirit by his Holy Spirit. How? Think again of relationship. The Holy Spirit takes the pressure off by restoring our relationship with God. Take a look at a familiar father-son relationship:

> Paul finished college and was ready to break from home and begin his own life. His father had a good trust fund set up for his two sons, so Paul asked for the money, promising to handle it responsibly. After all, he was 21 now and could think for himself. Well, he got the money and moved to another city—and proceeded to get caught up in the social life there. In a couple years, the money was gone. He then thought about going home, but he couldn't face his father! So he tried to find a job, ending up as a janitor with barely enough money to pay rent and buy a little food. He was so ashamed, he didn't even write.
>
> Another couple years went by and all he could think about was the mess he had made of his life. Finally, in desperation, he spent his last few dollars to take the bus home. He walked to his house, head hanging—his spirit broken. His father opened the door and stood a moment in surprise at the sight. The son stammered, not daring to look up, "I—I thought you might have some work I could do with your business." The father, with tears in his eyes, took the son into his arms and said, "You need not say anything—it's good to have you back home!"

Think of the prodigal son's spirit at that moment! He came back, pressured by guilt feelings and fear of having his father ashamed of him. When his father forgave him and showed that the son was worth something to him just the way he was, the pressure was off! He could lift up his head again and face his father. He could take a deep breath and see some hope—his spirit was restored. The burden was taken off.

Forgiveness, a sense of worth, and acceptance—these are the fruits of a renewed relationship with God. The fruits of the Spirit are love, joy, peace. . . . These are relationship terms, showing that our spirits are free and alive.

It looks at this point as if there is no escaping the intricate connection between *spirit* and *relationship.* Our spirits are most alive when we are sharing our lives with others. When, however, these relationships are strained, we feel pressure.

In light of these things, it's obvious that there is something very real in that space between God and ourselves and also in that space between other people and ourselves. That "something" is intangible and could easily be ignored by our scientific world, except that it just happens to be the most important thing in our lives. That something is the spirit of the relationship!

But what could there be in that space between me and another person? That space is empty—except for some air molecules. In a scientific sense you would be correct in saying there is nothing in that space between you and someone else. You can put a geiger counter there and find nothing. Pressure-sensitive devices will draw a blank. Electronic analysis will find no voltage or measureable amperage in that space. A search for special emission of x-rays, or even projected brain waves will be futile. The most advanced technological equipment will fail to come up with any evidence that something exists in that space.

But it takes only a moment to realize that something is really there—something powerful. Take a moment and picture two people in your mind:

> Think first of one of your best friends. Picture a person with whom you feel very comfortable, one you would be happy to see. Say that person's name to yourself. Got someone in mind now? Okay, put that person on your right side. . . . Now picture someone you would rather avoid—someone who makes you feel uncomfortable and tense. Say that person's name to yourself. Got someone in mind? Okay, put that person on your left side. . . . Imagine now that you are coming to a party

and just stepped into the room with these two people. Picture yourself turning to the right. You see your friend and your eyes meet. Stop it right there! You felt something pass through that space between you, didn't you? Turn slowly to your left and look at that other person. Your eyes meet. Again, stop it right there! The emotion was blocked, wasn't it? You probably tensed up and shifted your eyes quickly.

That something that passes through the space between you and another person is what this book is all about. That's where the spirit exists—*within* the relationship! The spirit is that which passes *between* two people, having a marked effect on the spirits of each of them.

Let's face it. Your spirit—your mood or your feelings— are tuned to other people. Your interactions with others become the fuel for your own emotions. You can try to defend against being affected and can pretend that you are not, but you really have no control over your spirit. It moves "where it wills" as you contact other people.

Didn't you realize how much your spirit is affected by your interactions with others? Well, think of the last time you were moody. I'm sure you can trace the beginning of that mood to some concrete interaction with another person. Someone probably disappointed you, ignored you, put you down, or criticized you. As this interaction occurred, you felt your spirits drop and the bad mood started. And so depression, frustration, irritation, and anger—as well as happy, affectionate, peaceful, and hopeful feelings result from contact with other people.

The conclusion is inescapable! The spirit of your relationships grows directly out of and is thus inseparable from your individual spirits. You are very much affected by other people, especially those closest to you. The way you are affected depends on what passed across that space between the other person and you. The spirit of any relationship lives in that space. Its presence when two people are together is quite noticeable—as is its absence when the relationship has become strained.

So, we know where the spirit lives and understand its effect on our own emotions and moods, but what is the spirit? We still have only a fuzzy picture of this concept. Maybe we have to search a little deeper to understand it. It looks like we'll have to pin the spirit down in more concrete terms.

2 The Spirit of a Marriage

L ET'S TAKE ANOTHER LOOK at Bob and Jeannie. We can list all the specific cues for the presence of "spirit" between them. Let's go back over the day of their first week's anniversary:

1. Their thoughts were pulled to each other often when they were apart. Bob would stop to look at Jeannie's picture and Jeannie daydreamed of being in his arms.

2. These thoughts were pleasant and accentuated the good qualities of the other person. "She is quite a person," Bob thought. Jeannie's mind was full of the pleasant times they had together.

3. Being together was more important than Bob's work or Jeannie's fixing supper.

4. There was an exchange of emotion when they first saw each other again—their faces and eyes were alive.

5. They touched, hugged, and kissed often.

6. There was a playful quality in many of their encounters with each other.

7. Laughter and other displays of emotion were open and frequent.

8. There was interest in what the other person had experienced and an attempt to understand.
9. The general mood was one of freedom, allowing the emotions to flow with free expression.

Now let's take a similar look at the tenth anniversary of Jim and Sally. Going over the same list, let's see if we can find out what was missing in their marriage:

1. They tried to keep the other person out of their thoughts by keeping their minds occupied with other things.
2. When a thought about the other person did break through, it was usually painful and unpleasant. Jim associated coldness with his mental picture of Sally and she felt anger at the memory of Jim slamming the door.
3. Jim found work more important than Sally and Sally's hurt feelings were more important to her than her relationship with Jim.
4. There was no exchange of emotion when Jim came home—only silence.
5. Jim and Sally never touched each other that night. A kiss or a hug was not even thought of.
6. Every interaction was serious and heavy. There was nothing playful or light between them.
7. Feelings were very much guarded, except for outbursts of anger.
8. There was no attempt to understand the other person. Neither seemed interested in what had happened that day.
9. The general mood was one of guardedness, tension, and pressure, keeping the free flow of emotions well under control.

Beginning to get the picture? There are definite, concrete cues for the presence or absence of spirit in a marriage. The two people act differently toward each other when the spirit is alive than when it has been crushed.

Now let's summarize these cues. When the spirit of a marriage is alive, there is a free flow of emotion between the two people. This shows up as they *contact* each other.

Picture the spirit as the *flow of energy* between two people. Imagine the spirit of your marriage as an electric current that flows between the two of you. Think of the spark that jumps across when a light switch makes contact. The flow of energy brightens up the room. Isn't this similar to the way a friend can brighten up your life? You feel a little bored or gloomy—then your friend drops by. You see each other. Contact is made and the light goes on! Your face brightens up and you feel your spirit lifting. The room is full of life now. The gloominess is gone.

Picture your own feelings and emotions as a generator. A generator produces electricity and can store it in a battery. When the battery is charged up, it is ready to start the car. Someone turns the key. Two points come into contact. There is a bow of energy across the points of the starter switch. The motor roars into life and the car takes off.

The same thing happens with people. Let's say that you are sitting at a school play, watching your child perform. You feel pride and many other emotions stir up within you. The generator has been at work and you are charged up with emotion. Then what do you do next? You instinctively turn to your spouse to share the moment. Your eyes meet and something passes between you. There is a powerful flow of energy. Contact is made.

This flow of energy describes the spirit of a relationship. If the spirit is good and strong, the flow will be free and will have a real spark to it when contact is made. So *contact* and *flow of energy* are the key words in understanding what goes on in a relationship.

The spirit of a marriage, therefore, is alive and strong

when a good flow of energy is present as evidenced by the following:

1. Contact is frequent.
2. Contact is easy and natural.
3. Contact creates emotion.
4. The desire for further contact is present.
5. Mutual understanding is part of the contact.

Let's take one final look at the two couples. The cues for what was going on between husband and wife on the day of their anniversaries can be placed into these five categories. See what happens when we do that. Compare what you read earlier about the two anniversary evenings with this in mind:

1. **Contact is frequent:** A videotape of Bob and Jeannie would show perhaps a hundred times during the evening when the two were in direct contact. Contacts between Jim and Sally? Well, you could count them on one hand!

2. **Contact is easy and natural:** Bob and Jeannie looked at each other often, touched, spoke, hugged, and freely interacted all night, whereas Jim and Sally had to force any interaction.

3. **Contact creates emotion:** Words like, "her face lit up with excitement" described the feelings that were flowing between Bob and Jeannie. "He felt the coldness grow in him" indicated Jim and Sally's guardedness.

4. **The desire for further contact is present:** There is no doubt that Bob wanted to come home or that Jeannie wanted him there. Jim would rather have found something else to do.

5. **Mutual understanding is part of the contact:** Jeannie listened closely to Bob's frustration with his boss and the understanding drew them closer together.

Jim didn't understand Sally's unhappiness—they were in two different worlds.

Now we have a handle on the spirit of a marriage! It is very real and shows up in many concrete ways. Its presence can be easily noticed—and its absence can be very painful.

3 The Spirit of Your Marriage

WHAT IS YOUR MARRIAGE LIKE? How would you characterize your relationship with that person who is supposed to be a vital part of your life? Do you look forward to coming home—or would you rather stay away and busy yourself with something else? Do you eagerly await the sound of the car coming into the driveway and rush to the door in greeting—or do you dread that time when the door opens and the two of you are together? Do you find youself wanting to share everything that has happened since you last were together—or would you rather keep your life to yourself? Do you want to know what has happened to him (or her)—or do you find the conversation boring?

How about when the two of you are in the car, going somewhere. Do you have much to talk about—or do you ride in silence most of the time? At parties, do the two of you stay with each other and share your conversations —or do you split up until it's time to go home? Do you sit close together in the evenings when you watch TV— or are you on opposite sides of the room (or even in different rooms)? Do you often look at each other? Do you touch each other very often? What is the mood like when the two of you are alone? Do you look forward to an evening out together—or would you rather be with some friends? Do you think that he (or she) really understands you? Do you feel cut down, ignored, or unwanted most of the time?

The spirit of your marriage is reflected in all of these ways. The spirit of your marriage is the motivational force in your relationship. It is related to how much you *want* to be together and to how much you *want* to share your lives together. It will bring the other person into your thoughts often and will motivate you to do many considerate things for him or her. Like a magnetic force, it will attract you to his or her presence so that in every way imaginable, that other person will be a part of your life. A song, a word, a picture, or an interesting experience will pull your thoughts to the one you love when you are apart. That person is never far from your thoughts.

The spirit also shows up in how you read the *intent* of your sponse. If the spirit is in bad shape, every word or action may be regarded with suspicion. The worst construction is placed on everything. If the spirit is alive, however, that same word or action is seen differently since the intent is read as a positive, living one. A period of silence is understood as the result of a preoccupied mind rather than as a deliberate ignoring of the other. A critical word is seen as an attempt to be helpful rather than as an attack or a put-down. A tender word is seen as an expression of love rather than an attempt to pacify. Coming home later than expected is viewed with concern and understanding rather than with suspicion and distrust.

When you know that what you say will be taken in the right spirit, it becomes easy to express anything that is on your mind. It is easy for the two of you to share things without the fear of being misunderstood. But if the spirit has broken down, you realize that you need to be careful about how things are expressed—and the flow of conversation is stilted and inhibited. It becomes difficult to express the things that are on your mind. Anything that is discussed is subject to misunderstanding and there is usually an argument after the first several sentences are out. What is being said will be taken as a criticism or a subtle put-down!

The spirit of your marriage grows through *contact!* Each time you share an inner feeling, talk about some experience, laugh together, share a sorrowful moment, or work through a disagreement—each time you openly contact each other, you give the spirit a chance to renew itself. A two-second glance at each other over your child's antics can be charged with electricity! The evidence of a tear can draw you close together when something sad or disappointing is being shared. A touch of the hand can be full of tenderness and love. Willingness to stay in contact helps overcome periods of anger, eases the path to reconciliation, and enables the spirit to continue to grow in your relationship.

You can check out the current state of the spirit of your marriage right now. Even though this spirit is in constant flux and will possibly change before you finish the following checklist, perhaps going through the items will give you some idea of the current state of your relationship. Since the list focuses on the feelings between the two of you, both of you would usually have a similar score on it. Both of you instinctively know what feelings there are between you right at this moment—they cannot be faked!

Assessing the Spirit of Your Marriage

Put down the number of points you score for each item and then total the results at the end.

I. Contact Is Frequent:

1. Think of the most recent evening when you were home together—did you stay near each other?
   a. We were usually in the same room and close together .... 2 points
   b. We were close some of the time .... 1 point
   c. We were usually away from each other ... 0 points

2. How often did you touch each other today?
   a. We touched often and hugged each other several times .... 2 points
   b. We touched some .... 1 point
   c. We avoided touching each other .... 0 points

II. Contact Is Easy and Natural:

3. Focus on your eyes—how easy would it be right now to look directly at your spouse?
   a. Very easy and natural to look .... 2 points
   b. A little difficult to have eye contact .... 1 point
   c. I would rather avoid looking .... 0 points

4. Imagine the two of you on a walk together. How natural would it be to reach over and hold hands?
   a. I would do it without thinking .... 2 points
   b. I could do it, but would have to force myself .... 1 point
   c. It would be very unnatural and strained .. 0 points

III. Contact Creates Emotion:

5. Look at each other (or imagine looking)—what do you feel?
   a. I feel quite warm and open .... 2 points
   b. I feel some distance and uncertainty .... 1 point
   c. I feel disgust and annoyance .... 0 points

6. Now focus on your voices as you talk to each other—what do you hear?
   a. I hear a lot of emotion, freely expressed .. 2 points
   b. I hear some guardedness and flatness ...... 1 point
   c. I hear forced expression and tension .... 0 points

IV. The Desire for Further Contact Is Present:

7. During the day when you are away from each other:
   a. I think of him (or her) often and wonder what's happening .... 2 points
   b. I sometimes think about him (or her) .... 1 point
   c. I am usually not bothered with such thoughts .... 0 points

8. Imagine that you just won a trip for two in Hawaii:
   a. I would be excited about being there together .... 2 points
   b. It would probably be nice for the two of us .... 1 point
   c. I would rather go with someone else .... 0 points

V. Mutual Understanding Is Part of the Contact:

9. Think of what your spouse has said to you over the past day or so—did he (or she) share any inner feelings?
   a. I know quite well how he (or she) felt about things .... 2 points
   b. Most of what was said to me was factual 1 point
   c. I really have no idea what he (or she) felt .... 0 points

10. Think of what you have said the past day or so—did you share what was on your mind?
    a. I was quite open about my thoughts .... 2 points
    b. I did say some of the things that I felt .... 1 point
    c. I really did not say much of importance .. 0 points

After you have added up all of the points, check your score against the following scale:

15-20 points—the spirit of your marriage is very much alive!

10-15 points—the spirit is there, but at lower ebb at the moment.

5-10 points—the spirit is weak and sometimes hard to find.

0-5 points—the spirit is in danger of dying.

Of course no one can accurately gauge the spirit of your marriage and the questionnaire certainly cannot do it for you. But it can give you some awareness of the current state of your relationship. I hope it can also give you some hint of the need to keep the spirit alive and growing. No relationship is so good that love and concern keep flowing all the time. We are all human and our selfishness always gets in the way. So don't be upset or alarmed if you did not get a good score on the test. It may just mean that you had an argument last night. You might score quite differently tomorrow.

But if you did score very low and that's the way things are most of the time, the spirit of your relationship is in trouble. If that is true, you both know it. You may be able to pretend to others that things are still okay, but every time you and your spouse are together, you know that something is missing. You can feel the tension and constant guardedness. You can feel the wall between you.

If your score was a bit low on the questionnaire, go back and take it again, imagining how you felt when you were engaged. Was contact easier then? Did you want to be together more then? Things were different then. Why is your score lower now?

To some degree, you might say, that is to be expected. Isn't it natural to grow apart after you are married? Of course, no one is going to feel as romantic or as close after the honeymoon is over.

Well, perhaps that is somewhat true. The romantic element will change somewhat. But it is definitely not true that the two of you must inevitably grow apart and lose the spirit of your marriage!

What did you do differently back then? What made the spirit seem so good and your relationship so natural? You had a lot of good contact, didn't you? You sat and talked—just the two of you—alone, without distraction. You went to places together, alone. You stopped and shared so much of what you did.

That's how the spirit first grew between you. You were

together often, lots of kidding around, touching, looking at each other, and hugging. Your relationship grew through such repeated contact which allowed energy to flow freely and spontaneously.

So what happened? Where did that good spirit go? Why did the feelings change?

Part of what happened to the spirit of your marriage has to do with the *habits* you developed. Kids came along, work got more demanding and many other things got in the way. You gradually developed the habit of letting other things come first at the expense of your relationship. It became easy to take each other for granted. You, to some degree, *stopped working on your relationship*. You developed the habit of routinely acting in a particular way rather than working on genuine, creative encounter.

Tim and Mary met in high school. He was the quarterback for the football team and she was the head cheerleader. They had known each other ever since their freshman year, but it was really their senior year when they started dating. They spent many hours sitting, walking, or driving while they talked deeply about their future together. During the months before graduation it seemed that they were inseparable. He would come to take her to school, they would sit in classes together, study together, and be with each other nearly every night, sometimes until well past midnight.

They got married that summer and were happy and very much in love. Tim started out in a sales position and their future looked very good. They still did many things together. But then, gradually and almost imperceptibly, their lives started changing. Tim's job became more demanding and he started coming home later and later. When he did come home, they would still eat together, but then there always seemed to be a favorite TV show, a meeting, or something else to hurry off to— especially during softball season when Tim was busy either playing or working as an umpire.

With all of that time on her hands, Mary began to develop her own interests. She joined her own clubs and often just went over to a friend's house to spend some time. A good opportunity for a part-time job came along and after much agonizing, Mary decided to take it, even though it meant several evenings away from home each week. Neither Tim nor Mary wanted it to happen, but over a period of several years, it was evident that their lives had changed. They still spent some time together, but they seemed to have less and less to talk about. When they were home alone, it was so much easier to turn on the TV set than to face some of the problems they were having. In fact, they could go for days without really any significant contact with each other. The spontaneous hugging, kidding, and chatting gradually started dying away. The spirit of their marriage was in trouble!

Doesn't that sound familiar? So many marriages seem to be plagued with this problem. In fact, the breakdown of marriage relationships because of diminished opportunities for significant contact has become a disastrous problem in our culture. We live in an age far different from that of our parents. Despite the many blessings of our technological era, one of the negative side effects of the accelerated pace is the pressure on the marriage relationship. Just as there was considerable pressure on a couple to work things out and stay together in previous generations, nowadays the pressure tends to split the marriage apart.

Think for a minute of the many things that can prevent the two of you from sitting down and having a serious conversation—things that your parents or grandparents did not have to contend with.

1. Look first at your pace of life and the schedules that you keep. Does this sound like a typical day for you?

The alarm rang at 6:45, as usual. Dick reached over to shut it off and then would have gone back to sleep, but Donna got up and pulled the covers off to get him moving. Dick immediately headed for the bathroom, disappearing for the next half hour to shower and shave. Donna woke up the children, made coffee, and set out the cereal. The children were ready for the bus before Dick finished shaving, so they just yelled good-bye to him. Dick then read the paper over a cup of coffee while Donna had her turn in the bathroom. He then left for work before she was finished. Only one word was spoken between them and that was good-bye. Donna then went to her job as a teacher. Donna and the children arrived home at the same time, but when Dick got home, Donna had already taken the oldest child to ball practice. Dick did a little work in the yard, pausing to talk to the neighbor, and Donna came back home to fix supper. They ate supper together, but it was the usual hurried meal because another of the children had to be taken somewhere, so there was no time for any real conversation. Dick had an early evening meeting to go to; Donna was on the phone when he got home. The TV was on and Dick became interested in the movie. Donna came to watch it, but got tired and went to bed before it was over.

The whole day went by without Dick and Donna looking at each other. They said maybe five words to each other.

This lack of communication is typical today. Who lingers for an hour over supper anymore? Where did the family discussions go? What about the leisurely Sunday afternoon visit with the relatives? In a very real way, the natural opportunities for good contact between husband and wife have been eroded by the rapid pace of our daily schedules. Two people living in the same house can go weeks without having to sit down and talk to each other. It is no longer easy for essential daily contact to take place.

2. Now take a look at the way television has affected your communication. The average person watches many hours of TV a day—hours that used to be spent to some degree in communicating with others. It's hard to carry on a meaningful conversation with a person interested in a TV program. Too often it goes something like this:

JULIE: John, we are invited to the Jacobs' Friday night, do you have anything going that evening?

JOHN: *(not taking his eyes off the TV set)* Uh-huh.

JULIE: Does that mean that you have something or that you would like to go over there?

JOHN: *(still glued to the TV)* That's right, dear.

JULIE: *(starting to get annoyed)* What's right, dear?

JOHN: *(still with the TV program)* Why, what you just said.

JULIE: *(angry by now)* What did I say?

JOHN: *(laughs at something on the TV program.)*

JULIE: *(really mad now)* You didn't hear a word I said!

JOHN: *(finally looks up)* I did too.

JULIE: *(a little less angry)* Well, should we go or shouldn't we?

JOHN: *(puzzled)* Go where?

JULIE: *(blowing up and heading toward the door)* You never pay attention to me.

JOHN: *(stares puzzled for a moment, then goes back to the TV program and a moment later is chuckling again at the comedian.)*

Has this ever happened to you?

Television has had a drastic influence on our style of communication. It is rapidly becoming more natural to communicate passively with the TV set than actively to share something with another person. Thus TV has become another barrier to the essential daily contact and communication that keeps a marriage alive and growing.

3. The high mobility of our culture produces yet another pressure on the marriage relationship. A person's deep emotions are related to one's roots. In the absence of close family ties and a strong sense of community, one's deep emotions are often frustrated in their expression. Communication breaks down because there is less to discuss and fewer natural channels to spark emotional sharing:

> Gene and Sally grew up in fairly stable surroundings and were married with many well-wishes from family and friends. Gene, however, found a good job in a large city far away from home and the couple moved into an apartment. They were very happy with just each other at first, but as Gene's job got more demanding, Sally found herself spending more and more time alone. She tried to keep up a good relationship with Gene, but her frustration and loneliness so often came out in anger toward him and he found it easier to spend more time away from home. As their relationship deteriorated, there was no one who cared and no one who would try to keep the two of them together. They did not know their apartment-house neighbors and their friends did not seem to be interested in their problems. In a real sense, Gene and Sally were alone with their problems without family or any real community to help their relationship. There was just no pressure to work things out and a separation soon followed, making their marriage a short one.

In an age where so many people uproot themselves for the sake of a job or better living conditions, the pressure to keep working on a relationship and the daily habits of communication that close friends and family help establish are no longer present. The natural opportunities for daily contact are thus diminished. And when communications do break down within the marriage, the family and community who could help to put the relationship back together are absent.

4. There is yet another, more subtle pressure that our culture places on your marriage relationship. The age of instant solutions and accelerated change tends to produce a superficiality of relationships. Intimacy, deep emotional feelings, and true understanding of another person cannot be accomplished instantly—such marks of the marriage relationship takes years of daily growth and sharing. Yet our society gives all of us a sense of impatience. We want the good relationship *now*, without the work and risks that the development of such a relationship requires. So it becomes easy to plug in and out of marriages the way we plug in and out of so many other situations in modern life:

> Mike and Cindy had both been married before and met through mutual friends. They seemed to hit it off just right on their first date and began seeing each other just about every night after that. They found so much in common and could talk so easily to each other. Within three weeks they started talking marriage and within two months after they had met, they were united in a quiet ceremony. Things seemed very good at first, but then Cindy realized that she really didn't know Mike when he exploded into a jealous rage after she danced with someone else. His reaction felt so much like her first husband, and suddenly all of the bad emotions from her first marriage were back. She tried to talk about it, but Mike took it as a criticism of him and walked out and slammed the door. Mike took a long walk, wondering how Cindy had changed all of a sudden. She had seemed to be understanding and warm— but now she turned cold and critical—just like his first wife. He felt like he was in the same trap again that he had just gotten out of. He felt so miserable and decided not to come home that night. Cindy waited up for him, but coldness inside her grew by the hour. By

early morning, she started wondering if she even
wanted him to come back. Her feelings had changed
so drastically!

Such a situation happens often. It is not easy to get
to know another person well enough to develop a relationship that can stand the rough spots of life. It's so
easy to feel close to someone while dating and both of
you are on your best behavior—but this is scarcely a deep
relationship. True intimacy is a slow process in which
problems are worked through and misunderstandings
are confronted over a period of time. Only then can
trust and commitment develop.

Given the unique situation in which we all live, it is
no surprise that so many marriages are in trouble. No
marriage, including your own, can escape the pressures
to split the two people apart and break down communication. Thus, perhaps more than any other time in his-
tory, you need to work on your marriage to keep it alive
and growing. And the key to working on your relationship is the *habit of daily contact.*

4 Developing New Habits

IT IS EASY FOR TWO PEOPLE to lose touch with each other. Busy schedules, TV, bad moods, and a host of other pressures can keep the two of you out of contact. Simply *not talking* to each other can break down any type of energy flow between you. The spirit of your marriage just cannot stay healthy without daily contact!

But such contact will not happen automatically. Yet other things seem more important at the time than sitting down and talking to each other—especially when things aren't going too well between the two of you anyway. So many things are gradually left unspoken until there is actually less and less to talk about. Then you have developed the habit of keeping things to yourself:

> Jimmy and Sandy both worked; he as an accountant and she as a journalist. Jim had a particularly bad day since a costly error he had made in one of his auditing jobs was discovered and he had to spend the whole day going back over piles of material to correct it. The customer was particularly nasty to him and threatened to

take his account elsewhere. Jim felt lousy by the time he got home, his head spinning with the encounter he had with his customer. Sandy, however, had several very good experiences. She had a bit of praise from her fellow workers. She was also given a very exciting assignment and spent most of the day gathering information out in the field. Both had many experiences they could share, but the conversation at supper went like this:

JIM: Well, you had a good day, I hope.

SANDY: It was okay. How about yours?

JIM: Oh, some minor problems, but I got them cleared up.

SANDY: That's good. *(Silence)*

There is always so much to share—so much that you could talk over. The habit of opening up to each other, however, has to be developed before the sharing will take place.

So, how do you develop a habit like this? The first step in the development of any habit is to be convinced that the habit is important. There are two questions at stake here. The first: Is your marriage and its spirit important enough for you to spend the effort in working on it? The second: Will developing such a habit of daily contact actually help the spirit of your marriage?

The second question I can answer for you—*yes,* without a doubt! After many years of working with marriages, I am completely convinced that relationships grow by inches through daily contact. As you take the risks of opening up to each other every day, the spirit of your marriage is free to grow. This book, in fact, is based on the premise that breaking down the walls that separate the two of you is the key to keeping the spirit of your marriage alive and growing. Such is the importance of significant daily contacts.

But that does take energy and also involves doing some things that do not come naturally. So the answer to the first question is one only you can make. Your answer depends on your values.

Commitment toward working on your marriage will depend on how much you value this aspect of your life. So before we go any further, we'd better pause and take a value check. There are many different things in your life that you can focus your energy on. Many of these things give immediate rewards—such as more money or praise from other people. It becomes tempting to sink your energy into such areas.

But sit back for a moment. What do you really want out of life? What sorts of things are *deeply* satisfying? What is it that can make you feel warm and good all over?

Let me share with you some of the things I have learned from many years of working with people's emotions. I have listened to many different shades of feelings —emotions connected with vocation, schooling, debts, sickness, etc. By far the deepest emotions I have ever encountered, however, come from the person's relationships, especially the marriage relationship. I have not found an equal to the power of these feelings. The explosiveness of jealousy or resentment when the marriage turns sour or the deep warmth when the spirit is there— these can scarcely be duplicated in any other area of life.

I have, in fact, come across one emotion again and again in working with widowed or divorced people that continues to haunt me. Once the person can lay bare the depth of his or her feelings, there is an emotion that stands out. This feeling is a depth of yearning for love— for someone who would care and take away the awful loneliness that is ever-present. Someone to understand, to care for, and to love is what the person really wants.

It was about halfway through the group session when Sarah started talking about her bad day. Tom had called, wanting the children for the weekend, and that had upset her. He seemed so cold and impersonal on the phone and that brought back the memories of the bitter arguments that came before they separated. Her anger came back as she related the conversation to the group. Tom had made some sly references to her "bitchiness" and when she started getting upset, he said, "Boy, am I glad I'm no longer married to you," and hung up. Sarah was shaking with anger as she finished. "I hate him!" she cried out—but then, after the anger was out, tears started showing up in her eyes. "What does the sadness feel like?" the leader asked. "Ohhhh," came a sigh from the depth of her body, "I've lost him. I feel like he has died." Then, after a long pause, when the tears began to subside, the leader asked, "What's the feeling like right now?" Sarah looked up with her deep blue eyes wide open. "I want him so bad right now. If only I could turn the clock back five years. I would crawl into his arms and ask him to hold me tight." Tears started back into her eyes as she got in touch with the depth of her yearning. . . .

The importance of such a relationship is easy to overlook until you are faced with its absence. So, perhaps you can't really know the horrible pain of loneliness and the depth of yearning for love until your marriage gets so bad that a separation is the only way. But then it may be too late!

So, once again, I ask: What is it that is most important to you? Imagine that your spouse is suddenly taken from you. What would it feel like to come home to an empty house—to have no one to be with each day? Do you realize how much you need each other?

God has blessed you with each other—a deep and wonderful blessing. Yet how lightly this primary relationship can be taken! Can you see its importance? Is your marriage important enough to let other things go so you have the time and energy to work on it?

Just pause for a moment now and think about your life. What are the different things you do during the day? Work, meetings, TV, work around the house, projects, children—the list is endless, but there is a certain routine to your life. You probably have tomorrow pretty well planned out for yourself. What all will you be doing?

Now, is there a specific time you have set aside for conversation? Have you put into your prime slot even as much as 20 minutes of serious sharing with your spouse? Probably not! You might expect it to just happen naturally. After all, talking with your spouse is not something that needs to be planned into your schedule—or is it?

You see, if you do what comes naturally, all of the other things will crowd into tomorrow and you'll go to sleep again tomorrow night without any real, significant contact with your spouse!

So we're talking about forming a *new* habit—a habit of daily communication and contact with each other that is actually scheduled into the prime time of your day. Assuming that by now you see the importance of such daily contact and realize that it is not just going to happen spontaneously, we are ready to focus upon *habit formation.*

How do you form a new habit? Well, it takes a lot of energy at first because the old habits always want to come back. In fact, it will take a lot of energy for several months until the new habit has sufficient strength to make it on its own. After about six months, you won't have to worry any longer because the new habit will then start occurring naturally. After about a year, it will be hard to remember what the old habit was like.

To work on a new habit for your marriage relationship is going to require a real commitment on the part of both of you. You must be willing to commit yourself to developing a habit of daily communication. This is something only you can decide. But by all means, if you are only going to make a halfhearted commitment, like, "Well, I guess we could try it," or "It sure couldn't hurt anything," then forget it! This is serious business and if your energy is not there to make this change of habit, then nothing will really happen. I have worked with too many couples where one or both were not completely dedicated to getting the marriage back together:

> I didn't have a good feeling right from the start. Sue called and said that she thought they needed help with their marriage and wanted to set up an appointment. I asked if both would come and she assured me that her husband would be there also. They both did show up, but Sue came in first and Pete took his time to get into my office. Sue started talking quite openly about their problems, and Pete started studying the pictures on the wall and reading book titles. I then asked them both where they wanted the counseling to go and Sue came back with a lot of energy, assuring me that they would work on anything that was uncovered. Pete did not volunteer a response, and when I asked him directly, he responded, "I guess that's probably the same with me." No energy in his voice—no expression on his face—I knew that nothing would happen. The sessions were good ones and Pete did come back two more times, but then he had to work late, felt sick, and came up with excuse after excuse until it was evident to everyone that he just would not be back. The whole thing was a waste of time!

So at this point, instead of a weak, "Well, maybe we could try it," a firm energy-filled, "We *will* do it!" is necessary. If this commitment is not there, you might as well stop reading now.

Well, you're still reading, so I'll assume you're interested and committed to working on your marriage. Let's get down to the nuts and bolts of habit formation.

First we will identify the habits that you must be willing to develop. Here we must be as specific as possible, otherwise the habit cannot take form. You cannot just say, "Well, let's sit down sometime tomorrow and talk." That's too fuzzy. Habits are specific and concrete.

I have two suggestions for concrete habits, one for a short-term habit and the other for a life-long habit. Let's take the short-term habit first, since it is really a booster rocket for the other one.

1. *The short-term habit:* Would you be willing to sit down and put something into writing to each other every day for three weeks? You used to write to each other often when you were going together. Remember how it felt to get that special letter? Well, it would feel the same way today to know your spouse has been thinking of you.

When do you write? Well, schedule it in—maybe even write it into your schedule at work. In fact, stop and find a time right now in tomorrow's schedule to sit down for 15 minutes and write your thoughts and feelings to your partner. Got a time? Okay, write that time down in this space: _____. Now check yourself—are you really going to do it, or are you going to let something more important take up the time you scheduled above? You'll do it, then? Okay.

Now, what do you write? Well, don't try to plan out what to say. Start with what's on your mind—just like when you were going together. Then let the thoughts and words flow and think of what is going on with you that you would like to share. Perhaps some argument is what's on your mind—perhaps an experience you just had. Here is a letter I wrote to Kathy to give you an idea of what to write:

Honey —

It's funny how my mood shifts during the day as different things happen and as our interaction continued.

Yesterday I had I guess one of the worst feelings I can have — TRAPPED! All I would need to do is open my mouth + suggest something, but something STOPPED ME! It's like an invisible force that cuts off my voice as I start to talk. I guess I have a REAL fear (stupid one, but still REAL) of how people are going to react to what I say negatively. So I end up not saying anything + waiting for you to suggest something. I HATE that in myself, but I can't overcome it that fast — it has a very long background!

Your reaction after the chorale STUNNED me — I was caught by surprise by your outburst and felt HELPLESS. Anything I tried to say seemed to make things worse. I felt clumsy trying to understand you and very tense inside. I felt for you + in had had tears in my eyes as I felt your hurt + my own helplessness.

I didn't really want to talk to you this morning as I took off when you got up (I did have to go) + the phone calls felt tense + awkward. I couldn't concentrate in my office + I wanted to be with you to get rid of the horrible tense + distant feeling I had to you.

My mood changed when Bob came + we started talking over Mom, etc. I started feeling close to you + gradually felt more at ease + relaxed with you — the good feeling that I've grown to cherish. I feel OK with you now + that's a where I want to be!

Love, Dave

The only way to let another person understand you is to share what's on your mind. Many times it is difficult to do this with the inhibitions that talking to the person face-to-face can present. You can usually be more open and honest when you are writing things down without having to face the other person's reaction.

To get the communication going between the two of you, the written word can act as an arrow that can pierce through the wall of misunderstanding that can so easily arise when talking to each other—especially if it is a difficult subject. So, when you start writing, let go with whatever you happen to think about. Don't worry if it seems childish or silly—if you thought about it, it is important enough to share with your partner. In fact, in my counseling, I have found that the little things that the person hesitates to say because they seem silly are often the key to understanding the problem—like the tip of the iceberg.

So go ahead and start writing without trying to put it into any journalistic style. Let the feelings and thoughts flow as if there were a direct line from your mind to your hand. Then, without inhibition, the flavor of your thoughts and feelings can be expressed undisguised. That is what being open is all about.

Do you think you can do that? Don't be surprised if you have a hard time when you first sit down to write. It is difficult to form a new habit. Your mind is just not used to expressing itself like that. It will require concentration the first few times until expressing yourself in such a personal way starts coming more naturally. Don't give up.

2. *The life-long habit:* Would you be willing to take a half hour of prime time each day to sit down together for serious, totally undisturbed conversation? Now, I'm not talking about the usual conversation that perhaps you now have in snatches or in your arguments or as you share needed information. I'm talking about a highly unusual form of conversation—one that has some very strict rules for communication.

But before I get into how this communication is to take place, let me review again how such a habit will affect the spirit of your marriage. I am totally convinced that a relationship grows through daily contact between two people—contact that allows for open expression (open flow of energy) between the two people. When this flow of energy is blocked and such contact does not take place, the feelings and excitement between two people disappear. At this point the spirit of the marriage takes a nose dive. Your desire to be together and the degree to which you are a part of each other's lives are diminished.

The more real contact there is, the greater the chance for the free flow of expression between you. Your relationship deepens, your trust of each other grows through better understanding, you want to be together more, and the spirit of your marriage becomes healthier and healthier.

Convinced? Are you willing to commit a half hour each day to the marriage? Is your relationship with each other important enough to you to put in this effort? Again, I can only assure you that such a habit will most certainly affect the spirit of your marriage. You have to make the decision as to its importance or value to you.

Assuming that you will develop this habit, and not just try it or think that "it probably wouldn't hurt anything," we need once again to get down to specifics. Like any other habit, it requires energy to get it going and needs a specific starting point and concrete directions.

You need to set up a special moment for this habit. This is like programming yourself so that you will do it at a certain time. There are two possible moments that you can choose. One is based on the clock. You could set a definite time right now—perhaps at 9:00 each evening— as *the* moment. When 9:00 comes, that is a signal for the two of you to spend the next half hour together in serious conversation. The other moment you could choose is based on something you already do each day without fail—then agree to spending the half hour immediately after that. Perhaps you could talk right after watching the news on TV if you do that every evening. Certainly you eat dinner together—perhaps this could be the special moment. Before doing the dishes, you sit over a cup of coffee and talk. Perhaps you could sit down as soon as the kids are in bed—this also could be the moment that works best for you.

Do you know what would be the best signal for the two of you? It's best if it could be the same time every day. Make your decision and write it down here _____. This, then is your special moment. Without fail, this will be the time for the two of you to sit down together each day.

One caution at this point—try not to miss a day, especially during the first few weeks. This is so easy to do, since there will always be something that will come up to interfere. A week can easily go by without the two of you getting together. That's no way to form a habit! In order to succeed, getting together *every day* has to be top priority in order for the proper habit to develop. You will need to put a lot of energy into developing this habit at the beginning—or else you might as well forget it.

You also need to decide on a specific place to talk— one totally free from distraction. Don't try to talk after you go to bed. Your body is used to sleeping there and this would make concentration more difficult. Stay away from the TV where your mind is used to tuning out and becoming passive. Make sure it is a place where the phone, children, or other people will not interfere. It also needs to be a place where you sit up straight so that your mind can stay active—and a place where you can sit face-to-face. The kitchen table is a possibility or some other special place that would make face-to-face contact easy and natural. Decide on a place? Write it in here

_____.

One more thing before we get into the specifics of the communication process. Start this *today* . . . not next week or sometime soon, but today. No putting off—no skipping a day or two, but start now and make the daily contact one of your top priorities.

5 Daily Sharing

I T IS OFTEN DIFFICULT to think of things to say to a person you do not know very well. Someone you have just met forces you to search for some common interest—the weather, politics, sports—for something to discuss. You assume they would not be interested in most of your thoughts and reactions to things.

Your spouse, however, is no stranger, and therefore is interested in the things you do and the feelings you have. Since you have much in common it is only natural that you will want to talk about whatever is on your mind. It's as simple as that. With such a directive, you should never run out of things to share. You see, communication of such a personal nature involves not only telling what happened (the information), but also sharing the significance of the event for you (your reaction to the information). Let me give you a personal illustration:

I was involved for 10 years in the training of ministerial students. My life had been devoted to the interre-

lationship of theology and psychology until the struggle
within our church body led to the closing of the college.
Even though our family found a very nice place to live
in Hickory, North Carolina, and I found teaching for
another college (Lenoir-Rhyne) exciting, I was resigned
to giving up this primary dream. There was a year or
more of trauma in making the transition and a lot of
emotional pain. Then to my utter surprise and delight,
the new president of Lenoir-Rhyne asked me to serve
on a committee to search through the purposes of the
college—especially as it involved the interrelationship of
Christianity and the liberal arts. It was like a dream
revived!

When I came home that evening my wife, Kathy,
asked what had happened. "Oh, I was just notified that
I am to be on a special committee to look at the purposes of the college," I said. "Looks like it will take
some time, but it sounds okay." She replied, "Oh, that's
nice. I hope you will like it. It won't take up too much
time, will it?" In the press of things, the conversation
stopped there. I had shared what had happened, but
failed to give Kathy the necessary insight into what this
appointment meant to me (its significance). It was
only when she overheard me talking on the phone to a
friend, telling how much this meant to me, that she was
able to understand my reaction to the assignment. Then
we had a lot to discuss and she could justifiably ask me,
"Why didn't you tell me?"

Do you see the difference between communicating the
facts and sharing the significance of the events? The first
can be highly impersonal, while the latter is unmistakably
personal. Relationships are never built around the first
type of communication. A deep relationship means that
you understand the other person and understanding involves the sharing of feelings and personal reactions to
situations.

This is why you should share whatever comes to your
mind. As silly and insignificant as it may seem, if it is
on your mind, it must have some personal significance.

Of the many things that happen to you during the day, the ones that remain on your mind are the ones that have emotional value for you. You may think that the event was insignificant, but trust your emotions. If you remember it, it has had the power to stay in your consciousness, so the event was important enough for you to share it.

Still not sure you will have enough to say to each other to fill up 30 minutes a day? Well, close your eyes and sit back for a minute, letting your mind go blank. How many different thoughts, images, and feelings wanted to reach your consciousness? Well, that gives you about 100 things now to share that must have some personal significance to you since they came to mind.

So, what stops you from going ahead and sharing these things? There are still four reasons you would remain silent.

1. The first reason for not sharing what's on your mind comes from inside yourself. For some reason you may feel that you *should not* be having the reaction or emotion that you do have. Guilt, shame, or feeling that your concern is petty would stop you from admitting what is really going on inside you:

> Betty came to see me because she was experiencing a great deal of stress and anxiety. She was a very religious person and was well liked by all her associates. As I tried to get her to talk about the things that were on her mind, she would say, "That's what puzzles me—I have no real big problems and I really feel foolish coming to see you." After several sessions of patient probing, we finally got down to what was on her mind. It seemed that the person she worked for and had to be in daily contact with continually dominated her.
>
> Betty would go into her boss's office with some of her own ideas, only to find that her superior had other ideas

and would not even consider Betty's thoughts. This was
quite a put-down to Betty and naturally aroused considerable anger inside her. Betty, however, considered
her feelings as petty and wrong—so she tried to ignore
them . . . only to have them turn into longer and longer
periods of depression and anxiety. Only as she was able
to explore these "petty" feelings of anger and take them
seriously as real feelings, was she able to work through
her problems.

In Betty's case, she felt that her anger at being put
down was both wrong and petty. It took her some time
to see the importance of these feelings and to see that
they were not "wrong." In fact, all feelings are extremely
important and are valid in and of themselves. Understood
correctly, your feelings are really neither right nor wrong
—they just are!

Take Betty's anger for example. It is tempting to say
that a good Christian should always be able to repay
evil with good and thus not be affected by the behavior
of others. This may work if you happen to be God, but
it is impossible if you are human! Part of your humanity
comes in the ability of others to affect you. If you are
so insulated from others that they cannot make you angry,
you would not have the capacity to love either!

Anger is a very natural, valuable, and certainly not a
sinful response to a put-down by someone else. Its help-
fulness comes in its relationship-building aspects. This
emotion prompts honest reaction to conflicting situations,
allowing for open confrontation of the elements that
would be destructive. Anger, in its initial form, simply
says, "You ignored me and made me feel like less of a
person to you." Acknowledgment of such anger allows
for better understanding of what is hurtful to the two
people in a relationship—and thus allows for healing and
restoration.

That is why one of the directives of Holy Scripture reads: "When you become angry, do not let your anger turn into sin. Do not let the sun go down upon your wrath" (Eph. 4:26). Notice that this passage does not say, "Do not become angry." Rather than the emotion being sinful, the sinful part comes in holding the anger in and letting the sun go down on your wrath. Then the anger spins inside and leads to thoughts of getting even and such moods as bitterness or hatred—that is the stuff that destroys relationships.

So once again—if for some reason you feel that you should not be having the feelings you do have and this blocks your ability to share what's on your mind, take another look at those feelings. See them as important in your relationship with your spouse—even if the feelings are not all that positive or noble. Value them as your real feelings and make up your mind to share them. The spirit of your marriage depends on such sharing.

2. The second reason for not sharing what's on your mind has to do with the image you would like the other person to see. Part of our nature is the desire for respect and honor from others—that they might think well of us. This is a powerful motivation! For this reason, you would naturally filter out what might be harmful to that image as you share things with your spouse. Especially, if you are a bit shaky about your self-image anyway, you would try to impress that other person by sharing only the things that make you look good.

John met Martha while at the seminary. She was several years younger than he and was very much impressed with his commitment and dedication. In some respects, she worshiped him, and before they were married, often dreamed of being the pastor's wife. Even after their marriage, she would sit and idolize his sermons and his obvious dedication to the ministry. John, of course, liked Martha's respect for him and found it easy at first to fulfill the high expectation she had for him. But then, as the ministry lost some of its glamour and John began going through some personal struggles —he found it impossible to share such things with Martha. Doing so would have ruined her image of him.

So gradually, almost imperceptibly, more and more of John's life had to be hidden from Martha. He stayed longer at church—the only place he felt free from Martha's pressure. He could only be himself when alone in his office. By the time they both woke up to the realization that something was very wrong with their relationship, it was too late. Concern for image had become more important than their relationship and had produced a superficial type of interaction.

There are many more ways to try to keep up an image at the expense of the honesty and sharing that are necessary for a relationship. Many men have a deep feeling of weakness and a threat to their masculinity if they have to admit some of their soft or pretty emotions. The male is supposed to be above getting hurt, and able to take it. That is why it is harder for a man (usually) to engage in such sharing. Too often the male image is at stake and then openness is difficult.

In similar fashion, a woman generally finds it difficult to admit feelings of jealousy or the need for security. Her image is also at stake, for she would like to be seen as being more independent or above such feelings.

In both cases, it is a matter of pride. Efforts to preserve your image can keep you from sharing some of the things that are on your mind. Such blockage keeps your spouse from being able to understand, and thus help you. It keeps a vital part of your relationship from forming—for it is just at those times when you risk hurting your image to share something very deep that the two of you can be drawn the closest together. The spirit of your marriage thrives on such risk—not on keeping up the image.

The impulse to keep things inside is quite natural. In fact, the drive to keep up your image (pride) is very much a part of your sinful nature. The type of sharing that runs the risk of hurting that image just doesn't come naturally. It takes help from God's Spirit to give you the strength to go against your nature. The determination that is part of your vision as a child of God allows you to value your marriage relationship above your personal safety and security.

3. The third reason that you would not share what comes to your mind is a fear of the reaction you will get from your spouse. When your feelings are on the line (especially if your spouse reads them as threatening), they can easily be put down . . . and that hurts!

SALLY: What did you think of the movie we just saw?

MIKE: Well, I liked it. It was okay.

SALLY: Did you like the way it ended?

MIKE: Yeh, I really did. It made me sad to see him left all alone with no one that seemed to care.

SALLY: *(almost gleefully)* What? Why that's really stupid. You really missed the whole point of the show. How could you feel that way for that so-called man? He brought it on himself.

MIKE: *(icy silence.)*

It's risky business to tell another person how you feel. Right at the point of exposing your deepest emotion you are most vulnerable to being put down and hurt. It certainly would have been much safer for Mike to be more noncommittal in his remarks about the ending to the movie. He was trying to express a sadness that apparently was close to his life—only to get that feeling labeled as stupid.

Now why would Sally put down Mike's feeling? There could be any number of reasons. Perhaps she was getting even for some way he had hurt her. Maybe she wanted to impress Mike with her understanding of the movie. Or, maybe she didn't understand the personal nature of Mike's response and thus did not mean to cut him down.

The reality of the situation suggests that you are running a risk any time you try to share what is really on your mind—a risk of getting that feeling put down and thus being emotionally hurt. That is a true point of vulnerability and none of us wants to open ourselves to such hurt.

But again it becomes a matter of value. Is the marriage relationship valuable enough for you that you are willing to risk being hurt? Your nature (sinful and selfish as it is) would lead you along a less risky route and thus rob the spirit of your marriage of its freedom to grow and mature.

It really helps to have a spouse who is sensitive to your feelings and will generally not put them down—a spouse who is a good listener, open and accepting to your feelings. If you have such a spouse, thank God and then tell him or her how much you appreciate this sensitivity. If the sensitivity is not there, don't give up yet. Such listening skill can be developed. How to do so will be the subject of the next chapter.

4. The final reason that you would not share the things that are on your mind has to do with habit. You just might be in the habit of letting your spouse start the conversations, so you let your mind go blank when you

are together. Or you might talk to each other, but be in the habit of talking about safe things—small talk with no in-depth sharing. Such habits are powerful and will govern your behavior unless by some act of will you force yourself into doing something different.

You can test yourself out right now. Go and sit close to your spouse and make sure the TV is not on or the newspaper in hand. Then look at your spouse—now check your impulses. Do you immediately have something jump into your mind that you could share—or is your mind blank at that time so that you can think of nothing to talk about? In other words, do you habitually feel passive (mind in neutral) or active (many things coming to mind) when you are in the presence of your spouse? If you feel active, do your own feelings come to mind or do you feel like talking about something or someone else?

Both passive and small talk habits present a sabotage to the marriage relationship. But just because it is a habit doesn't mean that it has to remain so! The habit may go way back to your childhood when you found it difficult to express yourself—or it may have developed within your marriage relationship without your being aware of it. Perhaps your mind was usually on other things and you only half listened to your spouse—and now, even when your mind is free, you have the habit of not sharing anything.

Well, you can change habits, you know. With determination and practice you can replace bad habits with good ones. As you share with each other, this will become your daily habit. As you grow in your understanding of each other, you find more and more to share. You also then find more and more you want to open up about because you begin to experience the wonderful feeling of closeness that comes when another person really understands you. That feeling is also a very powerful force—it is the spirit of your marriage coming alive!

Now, back to how to share what is on your mind. I hope you realize by now that what is on your mind will be specific situations that have meaning or personal significance for you. The meaning of the situation will show up in your emotions as you express it to your husband or wife.

> Tim couldn't get the picture of his oldest daughter out of his mind. She was waving goodbye as she went off to college for the first time—so that is what he related when Terry asked him what was on his mind. He found his voice quiver when he mentioned the goodbye scene, so he quickly stopped and pretended to be interested in the newspaper. Terry, however, caught the emotion and responded, "It was hard to see her go, wasn't it?" Hit by her apparent understanding and acceptance of his feelings, Tim let a tear come to his eyes. He was then able to express the depth of his love to his daughter and how it hurt not to have her around anymore. Tim felt much better after opening up and felt so close to Terry—the appreciation, closeness, and understanding were all there in the look they had for each other before Tim had to get ready for his meeting. The spirit of their marriage was powerful at that moment.

Now it is easy to express what happened to each other. The only training you need for this is the directive to keep it as specific and concrete as possible. The abstract stuff—like, "work gets me upset," or "you always nag," usually is not productive. Such statements are abstract because they are not tied to a concrete, specific situation. It is more productive (in terms of the ability of the other person to understand) to rephrase the first statement into, "You know, again at work today, Jerry took the work I had done, searched until he found a little mistake, then came back to chew me out about it while Bill and Joe were close enough to hear. That embarrassed me and made me angry at him for picking on me like that." Now you can understand better how work was upsetting after such a specific, concrete statement.

What about his second statement, "You always nag?" How can this be made concrete so that it can be understood and dealt with? I guarantee that no spouse could be sympathetic to such a statement, because the word "always" is a reflection on the character of the other person. So get more specific, like: "When you asked me for the third time whether I forgot to call my mother, I felt you were being unfair. I did not forget, but did not have time to do it up to that point. That makes me a little angry at you for not trusting me." So, couldn't you as the spouse have a better chance at understanding this more concrete way of stating the same thing? Thus, in this special form of marriage communication—your 30 minutes or so of direct communication each day—speak your mind in the form in which your mind brings it to your consciousness. Speak in concrete and specific terms because *emotions are always tied to the concrete situation.*

Then don't stop there—let the other person have a chance at getting a deeper understanding of how the situation has affected you. Talk more about the meaning that situation had for you. The meaning is always conveyed by a feeling—so take more time to share that feeling.

But how do you move the conversation to a deeper level? All too often, if you do express some feeling, the conversation stops there with the feeling only partially understood. It is only natural that your spouse will initially understand your feeling as it relates to how he or she experiences the emotion. There is partial understanding at that moment and it is tempting to stop the conversation, assuming that you were both talking about the same thing.

But, chances are, you were talking about two different things! The two of you have unique ways of feeling—like two different musical instruments that sound the same note with different overtones and timbre. Every person's emotions are fine-tuned to respond in different and unique ways. Thus, even though you can have immediate, partial understanding of another's feelings, it is only through further communication that you can ever really understand the other person.

> Throughout our married life—at least for the first 13 years of our life together, I just assumed that when Kathy (my wife) became angry, her experience of anger was the same as mine. So I reacted accordingly to her anger—and my reaction would have been appropriate if it had been the same feeling as my anger. Much to my surprise, I learned one day that she feels anger in a different way than I do. Our oldest son reacted against something she asked him to do. Kathy then got angry and snapped at me, "Well, are you going to let him get by with it?" I took this as a put-down to me and a challenge to my adequacy as a father—so I reacted with, "Why snap at me, I didn't do anything." Then I left the room.
>
> A little later when we talked about it, I got my shocker. When I get angry, I feel a lot of energy in my head and feel very much in control of things. So that's what I assumed Kathy's anger was like and reacted by leaving the scene. But then Kathy explained what her anger felt like. "When I got angry today, I really needed your help." "What?" I said, "You seemed like you were in full control of the situation." Then it began to dawn on me as she continued to open up that her anger was only the surface part of a more insecure feeling. When Kathy snapped at me, she was really call-

ing for help because she felt so weak and defeated at the time. I totally mis-read her because my own feeling of anger means that I am firmly in control of the situation. This difference in our experience of the emotion had caused considerable misunderstanding of each other up to that point. I see things differently now.

So, how do you get deeper and open up about the intricacies of the emotions you do have? Well, first you need to find a name for the feeling that comes closest to hitting home for you. There are thousands of words that can be used to describe your feelings and it would be very helpful for some of these to become part of your vocabulary. If you have not been used to describing or even thinking about your feelings, perhaps the following list will be of some help. It might be helpful for you to consult this list from time to time during the day to check out what you are feeling until you become more familiar with this area. And, perhaps, post this list and the sheet giving the six steps in the room where you meet for sharing each day. You can add words to this list as you work through the fantastic maze of your emotional life. You will need all the words you can get to express the different shades of the emotions you experience.

The next step recognizes that your emotions are also tied to your physical body! With practice, you can become aware of the physical characteristics of each emotion. Such characteristics can describe your feelings to your spouse. Different parts of your head, your throat, your chest, your stomach, your shoulders—all take part in your emotional life. It may take some concentration, but you should be able to come up with the physical location of each emotion! Such discovery is often very enlightening!

A further step comes from the understanding that emotions have energy value and will spark an impulse to

FEELING WORDS

DISTANT GRATEFUL

CLOSE DEAD-EYED ITCHY LIGHT

affectionate DOMINANT

fearful NAUSEATED DEPENDENT AIRY

Relaxed SWEATY APPEALING Soft HOPELESS TWO-FACED

INDEPENDENT HORRIFIED

THRILLED SURPRISED ANGRY COLD HAPPY

HUMBLE GRIEVED DULL LOCKED-IN Peaceful

BREATHLESS PANICKY CONFUSED

CONTEMPTUOUS Pleased WARM

Comforted DETERMINED POWERLESS JOYFUL

LOVING UACANT HARD ANXIOUS

DISHONEST OPEN Sunshiny,

HORRIFIED! ECSTATIC DEFIANT — AGGRESSIVE —

CALM EDGY TALKATIVE GRUMPY CONFIDENT

TENSE PROUD UPTIGHT IRRITATED Paralyzed

CONFUSED Empathetic AFRAID Silly BUSHED

EXCITED HOPEFUL THANKFUL EMBARRASSED IMPATIENT WEARY

RESENTFUL SEXY FRUSTRATED COURAGEOUS Timid

quiet INSECURE ENVIOUS Compassionate

mixed-up STRONG Seductive BEAT CAREFREE

GIDDY ASHAMED SUBMISSIVE TERRIFIED!

SELF-ASSURED Lonely CAUTIOUS BEWILDERED

frisky Content THREATENED Depressed

ALARMED Sympathetic BURDENED CHOKED-UP TORN EXCITED

do or to say something. Even though you can control this impulse, to be able to share it becomes a good way of communicating with another person. These impulses are related to some body movement and seek expression by flashing words or actions into your mind. And since this flash is easily denied and can be present for only the briefest moment, it is not easy to share. Added to that is the potential threat of sharing something so personal. So the impulse is quite a struggle to achieve and usually requires a good spirit within the relationship to be shared!

Another step in sharing your emotions is to try to paint a picture of the feeling. You can try a word-picture or analogy—or even try drawing a real picture. This helps pin down that feeling for the benefit of your spouse and helps insure a better understanding of the unique shade of meaning that this feeling gives. Any illustration from the outdoors, from the city, from the house, from animal actions—any picture, no matter how silly, that pops into your mind when you think of that feeling is worth sharing.

The final step (and these need not be all included or taken in order) is to try to recall another specific situation where you felt the same thing. You must trust whatever pops into your mind as you hold that feeling in front of you to find out when you felt that way before. No matter how foolish it seems, it is important to share the first thing that popped into your head because that is probably the situation linked to this feeling in your emotional logic. Keep in mind that your emotional logic works differently from your rational thinking! Your emotional logic stays concrete and ties situations together that do not seem logical."

In summary, there are a number of specific steps you can take to go deeper into your feelings so that better understanding can develop:

Toward Communication of Feelings

One person is trying to "reach out" to the other person—
to step into the other person's world—not to judge, ask
why, make light of, or to offer suggestions, but *to understand* the feeling.

Step 1. Start with a specific situation.

Step 2. Get in touch with a feeling associated with the
situation and give the feeling a *name*—e.g. lonely,
anxious, happy, fearful, contented, hopeful, sad,
sexy, confused, distant, detached, warm, excited,
unfulfilled, attraction.

Step 3. Locate the feeling physically and describe its
physical characteristics—e.g. My sadness starts up
from a tightness in my chest and travels up to
my throat where it gets stuck and affects my
voice.

Step 4. Describe what the feeling makes you want to *do*
or want to *say*—e.g. My attraction to you makes
me want to grab you and hug you—or my disgust
makes me want to yell "Stop it" and turn my
back.

Step 5. Give an illustration (analogy) or a *picture* of the
feeling—e.g. My loneliness feels like an empty
house—a big old house that has been abandoned
with the windows broken and the wind and rain
coming in.
Or—my clarity feels like a spotlight piercing the
darkness and looks like this:

Step 6. Mention a time when either you or your spouse
felt this way *before*—e.g. My helpless feeling now
is just like the time last week when I had to leave
just when the kids started fighting.
Or, my worthwhile feeling is just like when I was
young and my father would put his arm around
my shoulder and say he was proud of me.

The best example I can give you of this process at work is something that happened quite recently between Kathy and myself. We were leading a marriage retreat and were trying to give the couples an example of how such communication worked. As she tried the first step, Kathy came up with an incident that had happened the previous evening. She then went through the six steps in front of everyone and came up with a very enlightening insight that has been helpful for both of us:

Step 1. "Dave, I thought of the situation last night when the phone rang and a person you have been counseling asked if you were busy. I remember being upset when I handed you the phone and let you know I didn't appreciate the call by the way I gave you the phone."

Step 2. "I know that I had some strong feeling right at that moment and I guess anger would come closest to describing how I felt at that moment. But I wasn't really angry at you, but at something in the situation."

Step 3. "Let's see, where did I feel this emotion the strongest . . . I didn't feel it in the upper part of my body—no, it was in my feet! I felt my feet getting tense. That's strange. Why in my feet?

Step 4. "I know that I really wanted to tell the person calling, 'Yes, he is busy now with me.' But, now what did I want to do? You know, this sounds silly, but at that moment I wanted to stomp my feet! I don't know why I wanted to do that!"

Step 5. "The picture of that anger that popped into my head was that of a disappointed little girl who was looking forward to something only to have it interfered with. . . ."

Step 6. "Oh, now I know what wanting to stomp my feet meant! I felt that same way many times when I was growing up. My father owned a general store and we lived close by it in a small community. Daddy would get home in the evening and we'd get started with something when the phone would ring or someone would drive up needing something from the store. That's when I would get upset and stomp my feet—when they would take away time that I was supposed to have with him."

After Kathy had gone through the steps, we both understood better what the situation of the phone call meant to her. Her anger was really more a fear that I would get too busy and not have time for the family. As I understood her anger, I felt good inside. Before, as I recalled the incident, I was hurt and angry myself. Why should I get a cold stare just because the phone rang? But after I understood what the phone call meant to her, I realized how much she wanted us to be together as a couple and as a family. I realized that her emotion was prompted by her love for me and at that moment I felt very close.

6 Learning to Listen

A RELATIONSHIP BETWEEN TWO PEOPLE is truly one of God's greatest gifts to us. It is more than just the sum of the two people who happen to be together. Something more, much more is present as two people come into contact with each other. That something which is capable of making life heavenly and making one's experiences fulfilling when it is present, but which can make life a hellish experience when it is absent is the spirit of the relationship.

The spirit is a very elusive thing! Everyone wants to have a good marriage, but just wanting it will not make it happen. You cannot will the spirit into existence. The spirit of your relationship is in the hands of God—it is his creation, and a part of his Spirit! You may want it very badly, but creating the spirit of your marriage is not in your power.

But wait a minute—before you take a "give up" attitude then and say, "It's all up to the Lord." It is true that God creates the spirit of your marriage—but that doesn't mean that you need to sit there and wait for it to happen. There is something you can and must do—both in your relationship with God and with each other. You can and must keep the lines of communication open.

You see, the key to the growth of the spirit in any relationship is understanding and acceptance! These are just other words for love. Knowing that the Holy Spirit understands and knowing that God has forgiven you and accepts you just the way you are—these are the elements of his love that draw you close to him. To know that you do not have to justify what you have done . . . to know that you don't have to explain again and again . . . to know that you are a child of God no matter what you may have done . . . this is a relationship with God based on his love.

Being understood by another person similar to the way God accepts and understands, is a wonderful feeling. In fact, being understood and accepted by another person is one of the deepest and warmest feelings you can have. It makes you feel worthwhile, draws you close to that person and opens you up more. The energy is there—you then want to say more—you feel so close and in contact. At that moment, the spirit of your marriage is alive! There is definitely something flowing between the two of you.

If this feeling is so good, why don't you just naturally do what needs to be done to get that feeling? You did it at one time in your relationship, didn't you? You listened to each other and spent many good hours in contact with each other while you were dating. There was a good spirit then, wasn't there? Well, what happened? Why is it so much harder to listen to each other now? Why doesn't it come naturally anymore? Listen in on John and Terry's conversation—first when they were dating, and then after they had been married six years:

Conversation When Dating:

JOHN: It's nice to see you again *(gives Terry a kiss)*. How have you been?

TERRY: Oh, I've been having trouble with my mother again. She doesn't like me spending so much time with you.

JOHN: Why is that?

TERRY: Well, she has always been critical of anyone I've dated. I guess she doesn't want to lose me.

JOHN: I can understand that it puts you in a bind. You don't want to go against her, but you want to be with me, don't you?

TERRY: You understand it right, John. I wish you could tell her how I feel.

JOHN: I'm afraid she wouldn't understand. But I feel for you.

TERRY: I know you do and that makes it easier to live with the situation. You are so patient with me. I love you!

Conversation After 6 Years of Marriage:

JOHN: I'm home. Anyone around? *(sees Terry in the kitchen)* Looks like rain, I'd better finish the mowing.

TERRY: *(obviously upset)* Don't you even say hello anymore?

JOHN: *(comes back to her)* Well, what's eating you?

TERRY: Oh, you wouldn't understand anyway. My mother's on my back again.

JOHN: You let her bother you too much. Why don't you tell her off?

TERRY: She just called to criticize the way we're bringing up the kids. I don't know why you can't stand up for me.

JOHN: *(angry now)* Here we go again! So it's my fault now. Well, she's your mother, not mine *(slams the door as he goes outside)*.

Why is it harder for John to listen and understand how Terry feels about her mother's comments? What happens after two people are married that makes it more difficult to listen and understand—to see the other's point of view?

The reason is that the longer two people live together, the more each is vulnerable to the other. Another way of saying it is that the deeper a relationship gets, the deeper the hurt can be. For example, I instinctively know that the person who can affect my mood the quickest is Kathy. She could not do it when we first met, but as our emotions gradually rooted into each other (as we truly became "one flesh"), what she would say to me became more and more powerful. Thus, now that we are deeply intertwined with each other, it only takes a two-second critical look to get to me, emotionally. That's what I mean by being more vulnerable as the relationship gets deeper.

Thus it is natural to be more on guard when you know a person can hurt you so easily. And when you are defensive, you cannot listen to the other person. So it is natural to be less and less open to understanding your spouse the longer you are married. It is therefore also natural that the communication within a marriage breaks down— as natural as sin. This concept will be expanded in the next chapters, but for our purposes now, you need to realize that it is not easy or natural to listen to your spouse after you have been married for a few years. At this point, it is more natural (and sinful) to keep yourself defended and protected from possible hurt than to reach out to understand. To put it another way, after several years of marriage, it is easy to become so sensitive to criticism by your spouse that you are actually listening for criticism even when it is not there.

Look at John's reaction to Terry's problems with her mother at the two different times. When they were going together, he did not focus upon the possible criticism behind the comment, "I wish you could tell her how I feel." He could see this as Terry's need for support and not just a criticism of him. Yet, after six years of marriage, John immediately spotted the criticism in the comment, "I don't know why you can't stand up for me." In fact, all he heard was the criticism. John could no longer be open enough to see Terry's need for his support and understand her feelings!

How can John and Terry learn to listen to each other? It is possible to learn this skill, even if it doesn't come naturally. Learning involves knowing what to do and what to focus on and what to watch out for as you try to listen.

I. The first step in learning to listen has to do with your attention. You do have control over your attention. You make yourself attend to something even though you may not want to. Sometimes keeping attention focused can be painful, but you can do it if it is important enough to you. So first you need to make sure that your attention is totally and completely focused on the other person's world. Keep this question front and center in your head, "What is that person's world like?" Now what could make that so difficult to do? What could keep you from attending to every word that your spouse shares with you? Well, I can think of at least four things that would make your attention difficult:

1. If you think that what is being said is a personal reflection on you, it will be difficult to listen attentively. You will certainly want to tune out at this moment because it hurts to listen. Imagine trying to keep your attention focused on the other person's world if your spouse is saying, "I was really hurt tonight at the party when

you ignored me. You seemed to have so much more fun with Edna. In fact, it seemed like you two were with each other all night. Boy, the way you were making eyes at that person—it was so obvious. . . ." At that moment could you see beyond the criticism and understand your spouses's hurt? It would take quite an act of will to stay in there at that moment! And if you do—if you can really listen and understand at that moment—the anger can be resolved and your relationship can grow through it. If you stop listening, there can be no understanding and the spirit of your marriage will suffer.

2. If your own head is not clear—if for some reason there is a lot of internal "noise" in your head—it will be difficult to pay close attention. The noise can be something on your mind that you need to do or say, and this will make you preoccupied. Imagine that you have to give an important speech in a half-hour and your spouse interrupts your preparation with, "You know Billy, don't you. Well, I talked to Jane today and she had just heard something from him. . . ." Would you still be listening? It would be very difficult to keep your attention on your spouse when there is so much noise based on some of the baggage you carry around in your head.

If you have been raised, for example, in a guilt-producing environment, so that it is easy to take things personally and feel guilty, you have a lot of constant noise in your head that would keep you from being able to listen clearly. Any hint from your spouse that you might have done something wrong would immediately set off the noise—and you would find it difficult to continue to focus on the other person's world. So if there is noise in your head, wait until the noise clears—or else shake your head twice to clear it, make a special effort to go back to listening!

3. If you find what your spouse is sharing to be uninteresting, it will also be hard to keep listening. Now, why would you be bored with what is being shared? Well, there might be something more compelling for you to attend to at the moment—like TV, newspaper, book, or another person. It is hard to listen to someone if there are such distractions—and a touchdown pass will usually take your attention more readily than something said in conversation.

What if you just are not interested in what is being said? Well, at this point, all I can say is—hang in there. Interest is based upon emotional investment. In other words, if something that is being said arouses some emotional reaction, you can no longer be bored. So, if you have little emotional investment in your spouse's world, you will be bored with what is said. So, again, *hang in there.* Try your best to invest more emotion in your spouse's world by paying attention—then the interest will come around! It's as simple as that. The process of paying good attention is also the process of developing an interest! The two go together.

4. Listening may initially be hard because you are not in the *habit* of staying tuned in. You could very well be in the habit of saying, "Yes, dear" without really listening. And, as the previous chapter pointed out, habits are hard to change. As with the sharing habit, the listening habit is developed by being painfully aware every time your attention wanders—then forcefully bringing it back to what is being said.

I remember one point in our marriage when I was definitely in the habit of only half-listening. Kathy and I might be carrying on a conversation, but my thoughts were elsewhere. At that time I was deeply involved in computer programming—so at the supper table, I would let my mind think back over a programming problem while Kathy would be talking about something the children did. No wonder she got the feeling that I wasn't there much of the time! I would have that glassy look in my eye and stay tuned in enough to respond once in a while, but she could tell that I wasn't really there.

She finally helped me realize how often I would do this (thank goodness), and I then started the painful process of staying tuned in—and for the first few weeks, it was very painful. I was so in the habit of not being there, it was mentally painful to keep my mind on what was being said at the moment. But after those first painful weeks the habit changed.

Now its hard for me to realize what I was like back then, when I tuned out much of the time. I am also much more interested in conversations in general now, and find interaction more stimulating, not only with Kathy, but with other people as well. The habit changed—and so did our relationship! The task of keeping your total attention focused upon one concern—to understand what the other person is saying—is the first step in the listening process.

II. The second step to good listening is the double-check. It is so easy to cut the other person off before the message gets across. This is especially easy when you have lived with someone for many years. You begin to think that you know them so well that you don't have to listen anymore. After he or she gets three words out you already know what is going to be said and stop listening. This is called prejudging. In my estimation, about 75% of the conversation between married people is misread. It usually goes something like this:

BILL: I don't think I'll have time to take the kids to-
        night . . .

RUTH: *(cutting in)* Yep, there you go again, backing out. I could have predicted it. The kids are never going to trust you anymore when you promise them something.

BILL: *(dead silence)*

Ruth did not listen—she just assumed she knew Bill's mind and his motives. She had prejudged Bill and stopped listening. Sometimes we even do this mentally without saying it aloud the way Ruth did.

To make sure that you are getting into the other person's world, you need to double-check your understanding. A good way to start your sentence as a listener would be, "Do you mean that . . . ?" There are many other ways of saying it, but the intention is clear—that you as the listener want to understand better what you are hearing. This takes practice—it's like detaching from yourself and going over into the other person's head. It means that you forget how you might have seen the situation and try to look at it through the other person's eyes.

Joan was crying in my office one day as she talked through some of her deep hurts. She opened up with her anxiety over her marriage and got in touch with how worthless she felt as Tom's wife. She was sobbing when she spoke of her worthlessness and then expressed a depth of love for Tom along with the fear that he would not take her back. It was a deeply moving 15 minutes and I was sure that it had some effect on Tom. So I looked over to him and found him studying the books in my office. I asked Tom if he had heard what Joan was saying. "Sure," Tom replied, "I heard her—in fact, I've heard the same thing hundreds of times."

Tom was not hearing and, in fact, probably had not heard Joan for some time. He was so sure of what she was going to say that he did not bother to listen to her or to check out what he thought he had heard. I then asked Tom what he had heard. He said, "Oh, she just said that I never pay any attention to her and she is trying to blame me for everything." I asked him if he heard her express her need and her love for him. At this point Tom acted surprised, "You sure she said that? I didn't hear anything like that." I was able to get Tom to listen better after that and in a couple weeks he commented to me, "Boy, I guess I really didn't know my wife —I'm not sure I ever will." But there was a new spirit in his voice as he said that!

Double-checking is part of active listening. It is so much easier to share something if the other person constantly lets you know that he/she understands and is with you. So when you double-check what you think you heard, you are giving good feedback to your spouse and making it easier for him/her to continue sharing thoughts and feelings with you.

Active listening is the process of searching for meaning. The words that another person might say to you carry the pictures and feelings that are trying to describe that other person's experience. Passive listening assumes that the words mean the same to all people. Active listening, on the other hand, recognizes that meaning is not automatically conveyed, but is imbeded in the communication and has to be searched out. Double-checking is a way of searching out meaning.

> Larry was in a bad mood. He had a rough day and had the feeling he was on a treadmill. He felt trapped. Grace noticed his expression as he came home from work and asked what was wrong. Larry answered with an edge in his voice, "Well, what do you think? It's the same old routine, day after day. I've about had it." Grace felt herself getting a little upset and replied, "Well, do you think things are all that exciting for me?"

Grace was passively listening. She just assumed that Larry was including his home life in his feelings and her comment began an argument. Active listening would have searched for the meaning behind what Larry said. Her response in double-checking could have gone like this:

> "By routine, do you mean at work or here at home?" Larry then responded, "Oh, it's the work that's getting to me. I was hoping for a supervision job, but it looks like I'm going to be passed over—and after all I have given to the company."

Now Grace has a little better idea of what Larry meant by his first statement. He was disappointed and hurt by being passed over in a promotion at work and did not mean that their marriage was no longer exciting.

III. After you have focused your attention, listened closely to what you have heard without prejudging, and then have given feedback as to what you think your spouse said—it is completely natural at this point to react to what is being said. Well, *don't*. Now, remember that I am talking about a very special style of communication that will be just one segment of your conversation with each other. The other times, you can react all you want—but at this special time for sharing and listening, you must stop your natural tendency to react.

In fact, you will feel a lot of pressure to react to what is being said. If you hear your spouse tell you of a problem, you will feel naturally pressured to find a solution. If you hear some upset emotion, you will feel pressured to sympathize and then minimize the emotion. If you hear something critical, you will feel pressure to defend yourself. But each of these natural reactions will cut off your spouse from the attempt to open up to you.

Take the comment of Terry earlier in this chapter, whose mother criticized the way she and her husband were raising their children. Then Terry said to her husband, "I don't know why you can't stand up for me." Her husband, John, could then react to what she said and cut off further conversation in one of three ways. A *solution response* would be, "Well, why don't you tell her to mind her own business." You can see that such a response would go nowhere. A *minimizing response* would be, "Oh, come on now—you're making way too much of what she says. You're not her little girl anymore." This, too, will tend to cut off further conversation. A *defensive response* would be the one he actually made, "Here we go again! So it's my fault now. Well, she's your mother, not mine."

Even a sympathizing response is not all that helpful, such as "I feel sorry for you the way your mother treats you." Of all of the responses, this one would do the least harm, but it still is a cut-off. John would still not understand Terry's feeling, reacting instead with one of his own feelings. Terry would feel more consoled than understood.

John needs to make a response at this time that would not be his own reaction, but that would allow Terry to further explore her feelings. Deeper understanding could thus occur by a searching comment, like: "What does that upset feel like? Tell me more about how your mother's comments made you feel."

Such a comment may sound a little corny here on paper, but when a response like this is made, the sharing process is allowed to continue and to go deeper. You will then know when you really understand! When you have listened actively and intently, you will feel a closeness that comes with deeply understanding another human being. When your eyes start to tear, you know you really understand your spouse's sadness. When you feel warm inside, you are really in contact with his or her happiness.

At that moment, the two of you are truly one flesh as God intended for marriage. The spirit is alive and free to move between you. The emotion is shared and the two of you are in contact. The flow of energy is powerful. There is a timeless quality for this moment—a spark of divine energy is evident in that deep human contact.

7 Cooperation or Competition?

YOU'RE IN A BAD MOOD TOWARD EACH OTHER. You both feel like avoiding each other. So, what's new? It sounds like something quite common and natural has happened within your marriage. You have sinned against each other!

What is sin except the destruction of a relationship? It is the natural impulse to defend and protect self at the expense of hurting the relationship.

Bill had too much to drink at the party and he was getting a little loud. Betty started noticing his actions and was getting more and more embarrassed, so she went up to him and suggested that they go home. "My, oh my," Bill replied loud enough so that others could hear. "The little woman wants me to go home." Betty felt herself turning red as a number of eyes turned toward them, so she whispered, "Bill, you've had enough and you're beginning to embarrass me. Please, let's go home." But Bill was having fun with her and said again, "Oh, now the little woman is trying to tell me that I have had enough. She doesn't like to see me having fun." With that Betty felt a flash of anger and turned away. She was completely cold to him later on the way home and the next morning the whole house could feel the icy silence. Betty had been deeply embarrassed and hurt and she was punishing Bill with her coldness to him. "He deserves it after what he had done to me," Betty thought.

Bill and Betty both sinned against each other. In different ways they hurt each other and were then more willing to nurse the hurt feelings than to reach out to each other in understanding and healing. There is something stubborn about human nature that just doesn't want to give in at a time like that. I don't know of any person who by nature will give in in the above situation. The fear of being taken advantage of is just too strong.

Think over the last time you were hurt by your spouse. Was it some cutting comment, a critical look, or a neglected promise—whatever it was, you were hurt and reacted to the hurt. And how did you react to the hurt? First, you felt some anger—maybe in a disguised form—but you first felt anger. This is a very natural response and is actually a helpful reaction, not a sinful one.

Anytime a person feels put down—that one's self is diminished by another person—the first response will always be anger. The flash of anger starts at the center (close to the stomach) and bursts outward to the fingers and head and can best be seen in a clenched fist or in a fiery reaction of the eyes:

> Jimmy had just moved into a new neighborhood. He was excited about meeting new friends and shyly edged toward a group of boys playing nearby. He just stood there for a moment, waiting to be noticed. One of the boys happened to look his way and said loudly to the others, "Hey, look at the weirdo with the kinky hair!" The others looked up and laughed and Jimmy felt something like a knife go through his insides. His back stif-

fened and his eyes lost their friendliness. He threw his
head to one side and walked away with clenched fist.

There are so many ways of putting another person
down and everyone, no matter how good a person's sense
of self might be, will feel anger when hearing something
like: "So, you forgot that again!" or "Boy, that's a dumb
suggestion," or "Why in the world did you do that?" Each
of the statements carries a reference to the competency
of the other person and will always be taken as a put-
down.

There are, of course, many communications that are
not intended as put-downs, but because of some misunderstanding, are read as such. A lot of times the mis-
reading comes as a result of a vulnerable spot in the
listener that would make it easy for him or her to take
things personally even though they are not meant that
way:

> Mickey had always been an overweight child and from
> the time she could remember, her parents were always
> scolding her for eating too much. She had been on
> more diets than she could count. The boys in her class
> used to threaten each other with a date with Mickey
> if they would get out of line. She grew up feeling very
> self-conscious about her weight and even though she
> looked very good when she got married, she still felt
> too fat. Her husband, John, was embracing her on the
> second day of their honeymoon and made the com-
> ment he meant to be complimentary, "Mickey, you're
> quite an armful!" With that, Mickey stiffened and
> pushed away from him. Fire came to her eyes and she
> snapped back, "That just might be the last time your
> arms are full!" and ran out of the room. John just stared
> after her in disbelief.

Mickey was sensitive about her weight and in this
case, she read a put-down when John had meant just the

opposite. So whether real or imagined, whenever anyone feels that he or she has been put down, the response will be anger.

The anger itself is not destructive, but is actually very helpful. All the initial anger wants to say is, "You've hurt my feelings and I feel diminished in your sight." The anger in its purest form will force the other person to acknowledge the presence of the self—to be sensitive to your feelings and then to treat you like a person! And anger that forces such a reaction is healthy for any relationship. It keeps people from being taken advantage of or taken for granted. If the other person does not see you as important, there can be no relationship—so anger forces the other person to acknowledge you and your feelings.

Therefore, if there is little or no anger ever expressed within the marriage relationship, it becomes all too easy for the couple to take each other for granted and to become very selfish in the relationship. The relationship quickly loses its pizzazz and the importance of the spouse diminishes until there is little to the relationship except for a polite interchange. The spice of having to confront another *person* is gone and with it the spirit of the relationship.

Now, wait a minute before you draw the conclusion that it is okay to get into knock down, drag out arguments. I said that anger in its purest form just wants to get a problem acknowledged and if expressed with that intent, it has positive potential. However, if the anger is not current (that is, if the anger draws from past hurts), it can very easily be converted into a destructive form. Instead of a type of "will" that is being expressed or a determination to make the other person acknowledge you, the anger can turn into an attempt to get even. Such anger then wants to hurt back and this, then, becomes the destructive element of most fights between a couple. The fight then causes more bad feelings and results in the accumulation of more hurt that can erupt the next time a put-down occurs.

This is what Christ meant by: "So if you are offering your gift at the altar, and there remember that your brother has something against you, leave your gift there before the altar and go; first be reconciled to your brother" (Matt. 5:24-25). Paul gives a similar directive in Ephesians 4:26: "Be angry but do not sin, do not let the sun go down on your anger." Anger that is current is not sinful, but can be spoken with the *intention* of helping the relationship by encouraging the other person to value yourself. Anger expressed in this fashion is more like determination—like a steel bit drilling through the clutter that has gotten in the way of your relationship.

This is the difference between saying, "I've got some bad feelings toward you and we're going to sit down right now and talk them through," (determination) and "I've had it with your complaining—no matter what I do, all I get from you is one complaint after another!" (vengeful anger). The first is constructive anger and the second is destructive—the first is current anger and the second is anger held in for a long time that now only wants to get even.

God's commandments point out the many ways we can hurt our relationships because of this vengeful element of our sinful pride. We are always so much more adept at getting even and nursing hurt feelings than at using our anger to work things through. By nature we will fall into sin and let that aspect of our pride assert itself—because we fear that we will be taken advantage of if we don't get even.

Our relationship with God is a good example of the destructive nature of our self-protection at work. We are always uncertain whether God will really care for us—we continually misread what happens to us (like sickness) as a sign that God is not there, so we respond by slapping him in the face (idolatry) rather than wrestling with him in prayer (like Jacob did). The Scriptures are full of this natural, sinful reaction, from the self-centered actions of Adam and Eve through the mistrust of the Israelites when they built the golden calf. The first commandments point to those ways our sinful anger continually hurts our relationship with God. We do not trust his promises, but instead get angry when things don't go right and search for other forms of security that we can rely on.

Our broken relationship with God becomes the basis for all other sin. Without the powerful feelings of self-worth that no person or event can ever take away—without the deep feeling of God's love for us—our self-worth has to be shaky because it is then built on things that can be destroyed. Without the sense of worth that comes from identifying self as a child of God, every person, deep down, realizes that the sense of self-worth is built on the shaky ground of one's accomplishments. Such realization makes the person take the self too seriously—and hence take things personally because of a shaky self-image. The self-image wishes, therefore, to be defended and reacts by fighting back, getting even, or seeking revenge when the self is put down.

Well, we are all sinful. We all do have such vulnerable self-images that are built on our accomplishments and thus will take things personally and be hurt by each other. So the rest of the commandments speak to that reality—how our anger at being put down by others can so easily be turned into sin and thus destroy our relationships with each other.

Honor your father and mother. Failing to give some-one the honor they deserve is certainly a heavy put-down and there is no parent who will not react in anger to, "Make me!" In the same way, the hurt runs deep if hus-band and wife fail to give each other honor:

JOAN: Honey, did you leave the bathroom messed up?

JACK: *(sensing a put-down)* I don't know. You're the housekeeper.

JOAN: *(irritated by now)* You sure don't have any pride in the house.

JACK: *(angry)* I might if you weren't so sloppy yourself.

JOAN: *(louder)* Sloppy? Well, I must get it from you. You leave the bathroom looking like a pig sty.

JACK: *(yelling)* Maybe I'd rather live with a pig than you *(slams the door and conversation ends).*

Is there any doubt that Jack and Joan left with very hateful feelings toward each other? They both dishonored each other, called each other some pretty bad names, and the anger reaction was predictable. They sinned against each other in that conversation and the resultant anger was destructive.

Thou shalt not kill. Killing is the ultimate expression of anger to destroy. Anger that has been held in so long becomes the source of revenge. The course of such anger usually goes something like this:

1. First there is the feeling of current anger. If the anger does not vibrate with any old feelings, it will be felt as a flush of energy to one's face, bringing on an alert-ness and a lot of feeling around the eyes. Imagine, for example, that you worked for a bank and one of your

customers said to you, "I'm in a hurry—what's taking you so long? I'm used to getting better service than this." Such criticism, especially after you went out of your way to speed things up, would be a put-down and if this were the first time you were criticized in that fashion, you would feel current anger. The flush of the face would feel similar to embarrassment and you would feel like snapping back with something like, "I'm doing the best I can."

2. If this anger is not expressed, it starts backing away from the eyes and makes you want to avoid that person. Such anger is no longer current, but is still accessible and is experienced as a defensive hardness in the eyes and jaws. Imagine that critical customer coming back and again saying: "What's taking you so long—don't you know what you're doing?" At this point you no longer want to look at the customer. Your face is tense and you don't feel like saying anything.

3. Such unexpressed anger then takes a trip down your body. It will next be experienced as a tightness in the throat. It is still accessible at this point, but is much less current and consequently you tend to overreact to the situation. If the same customer comes back when your anger is at this point, you feel a strong dislike and the slightest hint that the customer is getting impatient triggers off something inside your throat that wants to say, "Why don't you take your money and choke on it." The anger now has turned into a generalized dislike for the person.

4. The unresolved anger next settles in the chest area and builds up power. It has the greatest potential for

explosiveness at this stage. Such anger is usually not possible toward a casual acquaintance—such as a customer, but represents a deep, long-standing hurt in a relationship. Anger at this point makes the person extremely vulnerable to criticism from the source of the anger. At this point, it is so easy to misread that other persons see a potential put-down in everything that is said. A simple statement, "Did you take the garbage out?" can erupt into an explosive answer, "You gripe at me one more time and I'll stick your face in the garbage where it belongs!"

5. The unresolved and deep-standing anger settles into the stomach area and is experienced first as a knife-cut down there and then finally as a coldness. Such anger is no longer accessible, but acts as fuel for getting upset in situations which in any way "vibrate" with the original hurt. This anger is years in the making and many times comes from a continuous, hurtful put-down experience in childhood (like feelings of rejection). Such anger literally makes a person sick in the stomach and brings out feelings of bitterness and disgust toward the other person. This is certainly anger that has turned into sin—there is no love that can survive such deep coldness.

6. The last place the anger goes and is put to rest is in the pit of the stomach. Such anger is murderous and comes from years of being put down without any resolution of the resultant anger feelings. Such persons feel as if they have been pushed as far as they can go. This anger is felt as a deathly cold hatred that goes very deep —starting from the pit of the stomach and then traveling throughout the body in a sickening way. Anger such as this can kill! A person with these feelings can be pushed

far enough to actually murder another person. This is the ultimate destruction of a relationship!

Thou shalt not commit adultery guards against the ultimate put-down you can give your spouse. Sexual feelings that are displaced toward another person gives your spouse the very clear message that someone else is more desirable. This commandment is not talking about the light emotions that can be shrugged off. A person's sexual feelings are always imbedded around the deep, rooting emotions and a put-down in this area reverberates throughout the whole being. People can kid themselves into thinking that it is just a passing fling, but adultery is really playing with fire! The depth of jealousy and hatred —the explosiveness of the anger that is aroused in one's spouse through adultery can destroy a relationship overnight!

Two couples had developed a very close friendship with each other over a period of years. They went on trips together and as the friendship evolved, found they could get into deep conversations with each other. One day they started talking about their sexual feelings and were able to admit some mutual attraction. They were all quite intelligent people, so when one raised the question of why the taboos over sexual expression, it became an interesting intellectual exercise. After a while, both couples were able to rationalize the feelings—coming to a point where they could say that being able to share the sexual feelings would be the deepest expression of their caring friendship they could make. So they talked over the possibilities in detail over the next months and finally had everyone convinced that sharing spouses would get them into a deeper level of friendship. So, one night they tried it— then all hell broke loose! The intensity of jealousy, suspicion, and anger surprised all of them—it was more than they could handle. One of the couples got divorced within six months—the friendship was quickly destroyed—and the other couple went through several very difficult years as they tried to put their relationship back together again.

Thou shalt not steal is a commandment that recognizes our basic selfishness. It is natural to think of self before others—even to the point of stealing from them or from the relationship to satisfy our own needs. In other words, we easily put ourselves above building the relationship and can steal time that belongs to the relationship to further our own selfish ends:

> Jim had made a commitment to Sally along with many promises to help and support her when they got married. He meant to spend a lot of time with her, but the demands of his job started interfering. Right at the moment the job was more important because he felt Sally would always be there, so he "stole" some time from their relationship to work late. The stealing went on for several years with Jim always promising that it would be different when he got his promotion. But then the promotion came and his responsibilities increased, and he found it easier to steal more time from Sally with long business trips and work that needed to be done in the evenings. His selfishness finally did the relationship in— he woke up one day to find Sally gone. She could wait for him no longer because she no longer had any hope it would be different. His sin had helped drive her away.

Thou shalt not bear false witness is also a commandment that pinpoints what can destroy a relationship. To speak evil of one's spouse to others—to put one's spouse down in a gossiping fashion is one of the fastest ways to hurt your relationship. Think of how you would feel if someone told you, "Do you know what I just heard? I heard that you were really miffed at not being invited to the last bridge party. Your wife (or husband) thought you were being childish about it when she (or he) told us." The image of your spouse gossiping about you in a hurtful manner would make you quickly resolve not to disclose any of your real feelings to him (or her) for fear of their getting spread around.

This commandment also suggests that we should put the best construction on everything. It is so easy to look at the bad side of what one's spouse has done or said—to accuse when there is another way of looking at the situation. In fact, a good relationship would mean that you regularly could see the other person's side and thus could put the best construction on the situation:

> Phyllis saw Greg come out of the neighbor's house when she came home one day unexpectedly. He seemed to act startled when he looked up to see her drive in and she immediately suspected that he had gone to see their neighbor. Phyllis had noticed that Greg had been extra friendly with her lately and was feeling jealous anyway. Greg came to her car with an innocent smile, wondering what she was doing home so early. "I bet you wished I wouldn't have come home," Phyllis snapped. "What were you doing over at her house? Her husband is not home yet." With that, she slammed the car door and marched into the house in an icy silence. She did not give Greg a chance to explain that the neighbor's husband had called and asked him to give a message to his wife since their phone had been busy. Phyllis had put the worst construction on the situation and created bad feelings in the relationship.

Thou shalt not covet is a commandment that recognizes the ease with which we compare ourselves with others—placing ourselves in competition. Thus, instead of enjoying the happiness or success of another, we get jealous and critical because we covet what the other person has gotten. This sinful tendency keeps many of the good feelings from being expressed and understood within the marriage relationship. Instead of the good situation being an opportunity for the relationship to grow, it can create envy and jealousy for the couple who find themselves in competition with one another.

In fact, competitiveness between spouses is a very potent reality in most marriages. The reason for the competition comes from the ease at which something good in your spouse automatically makes you feel put down or inadequate:

> It was a big party and Sally was the center of attention. She had just written a series of articles for the paper and everyone seemed to want to get her opinion about something. Joe was at first standing by her side and from time to time would try to interject some of his thoughts, but when it was obvious that everyone was interested in what his wife had to say, he moved away from Sally and started to sulk. He felt like a fifth wheel and his pride was hurt. When the party broke up, he was very critical of Sally, wondering why she had to dominate things like she did and telling her that she repeated herself too often. With these comments, Sally felt the warm glow of the attention she had gotten from the party turn to coldness. Joe wasn't interested in sharing her good feelings and she felt turned off by him. She so much wanted someone to share her excitement at that moment, but there was no one.

The competition or comparing that is done within a marriage can be destructive. Children have a knack of forcing the parents into competition by, "But daddy lets us do it when we're with him." Then comes the bad feeling of being put down—of being the "witch" of the family by comparison with the "good" actions of one's spouse. And so coveting rather than rejoicing with one's spouse, is a natural sinful reaction that does not do your relationship any good.

God's will speaks directly to our relationship in regard to these commandments and our ease at breaking them. "How often would I have gathered you under my wings as a hen gathers her chicks, and you would not," is the yearning of Jesus (Matt. 22). God would have us all be a part of the body of Christ, in relationship to him (Christ as the head) and in relationship with each other.

But we constantly place a barrier between ourselves and God by putting our energy and values into other things—in effect, we put God down as we say by our actions that a relationship with him is just not that important to us. And then, following that, we are constantly at work destroying our relationship with each other, like within our marriage. We put our spouse down and hurt him or her by our misuse of anger or by our gossip. Our pleasure, selfishness and greed cause us to sin against the other person. And when we are hurt, we are more ready to nurse our hurt feelings than to restore the relationship. It is so natural to want to get even.

So, when you and your spouse have sinned against each other in any of the hundreds of ways hinted at by the commandments, the result is a breakdown of your relationship. When you have hurt each other, it is as if a barrier has been put up between the two of you. Just think of the last time you were hurt—what did you do? Well, I know what you did not want to do. You did not want to look at each other. With the barrier in place, your first desire was to avoid each other—to break contact.

Breaking contact is another name for creating a bad mood and when you are in such a mood, you do not want to share anything. It's as if you are another person at that time. It's almost like a demon has taken hold of you. When you are not in this mood, it's hard to picture what you're like when the mood has its grip on you. It's another way of saying that when the spirit of your marriage is good, it's hard to imagine not wanting to be with the other person. But when the bad mood comes—then, watch out!

8 Understanding Your Unpleasant Moods

It was good to be excited about each other, and Tammy felt young again. They were away for a whole weekend together—she and David with nothing to distract. The children, the phone, the door bell, the dishes, the business—all were far away. Tammy and David chatted the whole way to the mountains, talking about everything they could think of. It was like dating again —it was so exciting. Tammy started tickling David when he was trying to get the key to fit the door to their friend's lodge and he, in turn, grabbed her and pushed her down on the couch in a mock struggle once they got inside. They built a fire and talked some more—about their life, about the boys, about their love for each other. Neither wanted the evening to end as they sat dreamily by the fire . . .

IT DOES NOT TAKE AN EXPERT to tell that there are good feelings present in this relationship. The spirit of the marriage is alive and contact between Tammy and David is very good. But then, inevitably, people do things to hurt each other. They hurt each other's feelings and the walls of self-defense go up

99

to nurse the hurt. When the walls go up, contact is broken and moodiness begins. Bad moods occur when emotions have been stuck at a certain point, no longer free to be expressed. A mood is a breakdown of spirit. A person's spirit gets stuck behind a wall so that it doesn't have free course.

> The wonderful weekend together now seemed like only a dream to David. All the close feelings he had were completely gone and he could only feel anger and resentment toward Tammy. Only two weeks after they had been away together, David had to take on some additional work at the office—so he started staying away from home longer. Tammy tried to understand, but when the whole week went by with David preoccupied with his work, Tammy started having feelings of not being wanted. So she planned a good Friday night for just the two of them, but no sooner had David walked in the door (late at that) than the phone rang. There had to be an emergency meeting, David tried to explain to her, but Tammy did not even hear the rest. She felt numb as he left, and he felt guilty for leaving her. She was in bed, crying when he came in and when he tried to talk to her, she snapped, "So now you will pay attention to me when we are in bed." David caught the sharp edge of that comment, took a deep breath and left the room in silence. He spent the night on the couch.

Think back to the last time you were in a bad mood—or are you in one right now? Can you remember the exact moment you felt the mood come on? Chances are that the mood had something to do with an interaction with family or a very close friend—these are the only people who can affect you in that manner. And of the people who can really get to you, it is probably your spouse who can affect your mood the fastest because that's where so many of your emotions live. The wall

goes up fastest when you know you can get hurt—and
your spouse knows what to say and do to get to you!
That's the nature of getting to know each other.

> I remember getting into a mood yesterday (Sunday)
> morning. The time had changed, so we set our clocks
> back an hour and woke up early for church. With the
> free time, we started talking about costumes for Hal-
> loween. In the past, I have promised to help on the
> costumes, but usually waited until the last minute to
> slap something together. So, this has been a "sore" sub-
> ject. This year I resolved to do things ahead of time
> and we were hard at work making a robot-computer
> costume out of cardboard and tinfoil. Just as we were
> about to begin cutting, Kathy made a comment that
> reflected her past hurt over my negligence in this area:
> "Sure, this sounds good, but the box you're going to
> use is too small. His shoulders will bend it out of shape
> and the whole thing will look slapped-together as
> usual." That hit home! I felt unjustly put down at a
> time when I was sincerely trying to do things right for
> a change, and at that moment, I felt my mood slip. I
> had been excited about the project up until then, but
> proceeded more mechanically after that. I snapped at
> the boys for doing this and that and generally was in a
> bad humor on the way to church.

That's usually how a mood begins—a put-down or an
attack at a vulnerable spot. A criticism right at the point
of an insecure feeling by one's spouse will do it every
time. A knife-like reminder, especially with "never" or
"always" slipped in, will put up the walls. The hurt goes
deep and with the wall up, a mood sets in. Thus a mood
can be defined as the blockage of energy (or flow of
emotions) due to the presence of a wall in the relationship. In other words, a mood refers to getting all stirred
up inside without any place for the emotion to go. The
person gets stuck in a spot and sulks, pouts, or smolders.
That's a mood.

When you are in a mood, you can feel the walls around you. You know what it's like. Things seem to close in on you and you have a "knotted up" feeling—the lack of energy to do anything. If your spouse was responsible for the wall, you do not want any contact with him or her. You avoid looking at your spouse's eyes. Touching is out of the question, so you don't feel like getting within four feet of the other person. Direct conversation is even undesirable, so if your spouse asks a question, you either ignore it or grunt the briefest reply possible in clipped, robot-like language. You just do not want contact.

> It had been weeks since Joe and Sarah had spoken to each other. They still lived in the same house, but that was about it. They slept in separate bedrooms and carefully stayed in different parts of the house. If Joe was watching TV, Sarah would be doing something upstairs—and if Sarah was in the den, Joe would find something to do in the garage. They even got into the habit of writing little, terse notes and putting them on the steering wheels of their separate cars. Joe and Sarah were totally out of contact—the mood was so thick in their house that you could almost cut it. The wall was so easy to see and feel. The spirit of their marriage was in bad shape.

You can usually tell if you are in the slightest mood by your eyes. If the wall is present in the least, you will have some trouble looking directly into your spouse's eyes. If you have even the slightest hesitation, the wall is there and the mood is present.

Think of a little child. It's so much easier to see how the mood works:

> Billy was looking forward to going to the movie, *Star Wars*, with his father. He had been after his parents to take him for several weeks and finally his father thought that Saturday afternoon would be a possibility.

All week Billy was looking forward to Saturday and had told all his friends at school that he was going. But then Saturday came and Daddy suddenly got busy. Billy asked him Saturday morning when they were going and his father said that they couldn't go this weekend. "But you promised," Billy started, but then got cut off with a stern, "Don't talk back—I said we were not going this weekend and that's final," from father. With that his hopes were dashed—his needs had been put down and the lower lip went out into a pout. Bill turned away with a tear in his eye and went to his room. His father realized he had come on too strong, and, feeling guilty, went in after Billy. "Come on, Billy, it's not the end of the world," his father tried. Billy just went "Mmmmmpp" and buried his head in the pillow.

Now, why didn't Billy want to get into contact with his father? Well, he instinctively knew that if he did re-establish contact, the mood would be broken and he felt he deserved to stay in that mood for awhile. He had been hurt and pouting was a way of getting even. He had to punish his father adequately—this is what the mood was all about. It was designed to make his father feel guilty.

In the same way—in a crazy way—when you get into a mood, you don't want to get out too fast. If you do, it's like giving in and letting the other person win. When you have been hurt, you feel that you deserve a good pout—letting the person feel guilty about putting you down. So the wall goes up—you do not feel like looking at your spouse—and there is tension around the house.

But this is natural and inevitable. You really can't stop hurting each other and you really don't have control over getting into a mood or not. When you have been hurt in one of your vulnerable spots, you will put the wall up. Trying to stop things up to this point will be like trying to dam up the ocean. It will happen, no matter how hard

you try to stop it—it will happen if you are both vulnerable to each other. If you just have a polite relationship
(surface one), then perhaps you can keep from getting
put into a mood. But if there is life in your marriage and
if the emotions are free to flow, a mood is inevitable.

So the concern here is what to do *when* the mood
occurs. This is something you can attend to—to break
down the wall and get back into contact when things are
tense. This will be the focus of the next chapter.

So, before we get to the "how to restore" portion of
the book, let's take a closer look at what makes up the
wall that creates the mood and keeps the two of you out
of contact. A closer look at the wall reveals that it is
made up of two layers of bricks. This is to indicate that
both people are responsible for building up the wall. In
other words, the breakdown of a relationship is never
caused by one person—there is always a double layer of
bricks on the wall.

One layer may be much more subtle, but with a little
probing, it will make itself known:

> Pete was liked by everyone. He always had a kind
> word and a helping hand when someone needed him.
> He was gentle and never seemed to get angry—always
> concerned about the other person—the perfect Chris-
> tian, so everyone said. Julie was much the opposite and
> constantly felt bad about what she had done. She would
> land into Pete and almost go hysterical as she tried to
> get to him, but he would just smile and ask her what
> was wrong, so he could do something about it. It looked
> like she was the witch and he was the nice guy. She
> continued to cut at him, and on the surface it looked
> like the breakdown of their relationship had to do with
> the bricks she put up by landing into him for seemingly
> petty things. But a closer look revealed an equal num-
> ber of bricks on Pete's side of the wall. He had cut
> Julie off many times from his feelings and her "bitchi-
> ness" was a desperate attempt on her part to contact

him. His subtle wall of "kindness" really kept him out of contact with Julie and had the effect of making her appear to be the "bad" person for always bringing up things.

I guess that this is just another way of saying that "all have sinned and fallen short" (Rom. 3:23). In any broken relationship, the wall is made up of the sins of both persons. Oh, I know that each of the persons involved would like to think that it was primarily the other person's fault —we all want to justify our actions. And it is so much easier to see the mote in the other person's eye than the beam in our own eye.

Still not convinced? Still like to try to find out who is at fault in the broken relationship? Well, let's try another example.

Jerry promised not to drink anymore. He said that he realized that it was hurting the family and he would stop. Suzie didn't really believe him, but since he had promised so strongly, she said okay. He didn't touch a drink for two weeks, but then one night, he came home feeling tense. He was preoccupied and did not feel good at all. Suzie asked him if he had been drinking again and even though he said that he had not, she kept after him, accusing him of having a hangover. With her suspicion and accusation, the pressure mounted in his head until he just had to slip out of the house. But then, the next thing he knew, he was in a bar—but didn't care any longer. The awful pressure was gone. When he came home very drunk, Suzie's worst fears were confirmed—he did not keep his promise and she resolved never to trust him again.

Was Jerry the bad person? Sure, he had sinned against the relationship by not confronting the situation and by turning everything off with alcohol. But what about Suzie? How many times was she willing to forgive—

certainly not 70 times 7. Looking a little closer, she did not seek to understand her husband, but only added to the pressure by her fear of being hurt again—in fact, this fear of being hurt really helped set up the situation.

It probably would not be humanly possible for Suzie to continue to forgive Jerry. In fact, it would probably be best for her to confront the problem, rather than to just "forgive" and pass over. But to do the right thing in that situation at all times is humanly impossible. So the inevitable will occur. Just as Jerry sinned against the relationship by his drinking, so also will Suzie sin against the relationship by her nagging, lack of trust, and not wanting to feel like a fool by trying to understand. That the two will sin against each other and hurt the relationship with the subsequent wall that will form is inevitable! Sin is a daily reality in all relationships.

The conclusion is clear. In every broken relationship, the bricks that put the wall up are piled two deep. Both need to confront the bricks that they put up first before anything else can be done for the relationship. Both need to confess to each other! If for example, Jerry is forced to take all the blame, he will never be able to come back fully into the relationship—he would no longer be able to function as a person and if he did come back, part of him would be missing.

Picture again in your mind a brick wall. Notice that the bricks will fall down easily unless they are held in place by mortar. When a person has been put down in the relationship—when there has been a real or imagined hurt—something automatically comes between the two people. This can be conceived of as the brick itself. The hard brick is actually the natural reaction of anger toward being put down. When this anger is expressed in its pure form and is then acknowledged by the other person, the brick is knocked down and is gone. That hurtful situation will no longer be remembered and whatever it put between two people will be gone.

Betsy wasn't feeling very well anyway. She had taken care of two sick children for a whole week with her husband gone. Randy had just come home and she was looking for someone to help her and be with her. It had been a lonely, tiring week. Both kids were crying when Randy walked in. He had been on the go for a solid week without sitting down to rest. He was looking forword to some peace and quiet at home. He put up with the noise and confusion for about 20 minutes, trying to talk to Betsy in bits and pieces—picking up some negative vibrations from her for his being gone. Then he snapped, "What in the world is wrong with these children, anyway?" It sounded like an accusation to Betsy and she burst into tears—the wall went up in a hurry. Her mood was completely changed.

As Betsy lapsed into silence, Randy felt like going back out the door. The mood was getting worse by the minute and he was upset and tired. Instead, he took a deep breath, turned to Betsy and said, "Hey, let's stop and let everything else go and talk this over." Betsy really didn't want to, but finally agreed and they sat down together. In tears Betsy told him how much she looked forward to his coming home and how she needed him—then when Randy understood and explained that his snappy comment came out of his pressure and was not meant to accuse her, the mood lifted. Ten minutes later Randy and Betsy were laughing at something that had happened earlier in the week. The wall was gone and the mood was good again as they were once more in contact.

When Betsy and Randy sat down to talk about their feelings, the brick that had just been put into place, was dislodged and the wall came tumbling down. But if the brick remains in place for any length of time, the mortar that helped put it in place starts to harden and the brick becomes harder and harder to remove.

Anger that is held in for a time, as we have seen before, turns into the destructive emotions of bitterness, disgust, and hate. It prompts you to get even and to somehow get back at that person who hurt you. Once the wall is up, the feelings have no place to go and they build up in intensity. Then, when the intensity is sufficiently strong, a person can come to the point where a minor incident finally prompts the feeling that "I've had it up to here."

> Ned had spent a lot of time picking out Jane's birthday present. He was nervous about it and tried to find something she would like—so he picked out a birthstone ring. He gave it to her in the bedroom and was excited as she started opening it. But when she saw the ring, she gave him a disgusted look and asked, "What in the world made you get this dumb thing?" With that, Ned saw red. He felt all of the emotion collect in his face and he said icily, "I've had it with you." With that he walked out and started separation procedures. He had really had it!

But what had he had? The angry emotions that he had collected over a long period of time behind the wall in their relationship finally got too strong. The wall had gotten too high for any good contact to occur between Jane and Ned. With that last incident—which certainly could not have prompted such a drastic move as separation—the last trace of the spirit of their marriage was killed. Ned no longer had any desire to work on the marriage. The wall was just too high and the mortar too solidified to try anymore.

When you hurt each other and become upset, it is quite natural to try to ignore the feelings. When you do ignore the hurt, it will seem to go away—but it actually won't. The wall that was built by the hurt will still be there, even though you consciously avoid the subject. Yet, just as soon as the subject is brought up again, you automatically remember any unresolved hurt or any unfinished business. So, when there is a wall of hurt in your relationship that has not been talked through, then you have to avoid many subjects and steer clear of so many emotional areas until finally there is very little emotion left in your marriage—until the spirit-flow is no longer there and your desire to be with each other is gone. The wall will stay intact until the bricks are confronted and knocked away.

It's like a cycle that your marriage gets into. One of you hurts the other (real or imagined) and the natural result is some hurt in return. This causes more hard feelings and a reciprocal attempt to hurt or put down. Then the cycle becomes more vicious and continues on and on. With such a cycle over a period of years, a good marriage relationship can be destroyed. As the wall goes higher and higher, the spirit of the marriage gets weaker and weaker until that point when it dies—when you've "had it up to here."

9 Confronting the Wall

REMEMBER THAT A MOOD CAN HAPPEN only when you are out of contact. *Restoring contact breaks the mood*—it's as simple as that. You don't have to solve your differences—just break through the *wall* and come back into contact.

As we have seen, from the beginning of your marriage relationship, a wall has started building up between the two of you. Each day, as both of you feel slighted, misunderstood, upset, embarrassed, or in some other way hurt by your spouse, you add a brick to that wall. You can't help it. It is part of your human nature to pout, carry a grudge, and want to get even. Each time you feel that way to your mate, you place another brick on the wall. Each brick slows down the energy-flow and if allowed to stand, destroys the spirit of your marriage.

It is actually easy to tell when the bricks are there. Your eyes give you away. If there is hesitancy in looking at each other, something is wrong between you. There are some bricks getting in the way that represent unresolved conflicts. If they are ignored, they will not go away.

Direct confrontation of the wall in the presence of each other is the way to break down the wall. Time will seem to heal the wounds, but time can only transfer the wall into the unconscious. It will still be there, but less accessible. The hurt comes back in a flash of disgust or anger. It accompanies the next hurt, causing you to overreact to your spouse over a relatively minor incident.

It is not easy to confront the wall that is between you. When you are hurt, it is natural for you to pout. In fact, you want to make life miserable for your mate by getting into a mood and not letting on what is wrong. The mood itself is, in a perverse way, enjoyable. You feel justified in nursing the mood and making life hard for your spouse. The last thing you feel like doing when in such a mood is to make contact with your spouse, because you know that such direct contact can break that mood and rob you of the sinful pleasure of revenge.

So, when there is something between the two of you, you must overcome the natural urge to avoid contact. Sometimes it takes every ounce of your willpower to do so, but such confrontation is essential to the relationship. Especially when the two of you have been hurt deeply by each other, it is natural to be defensive, expecting the other person to use anything you may say against you. It is so much easier to blame the other person for what has happened than to swallow your pride and admit that you helped build up 50% of the wall! It is always his fault for running around or failing to pay attention or her fault for nagging so much or being cold and inaccessible.

To struggle for reconcilation means that the two people are able to overcome the desire to withdraw or to hurt back. Painfully, with feelings of being foolish and awkward, the couple must *confront each other with the intent to restore the relationship!*

> Mary had a hard time with her emotions. Dick had an affair and had treated her badly when she found out about it. She therefore felt justified in punishing him for it. After coming very close to divorce, both Dick and Mary showed each other that they *intended* to help the relationship by their willingness to seek counsel. Dick's struggle after that became one of stopping his natural impulse to defend himself by withdrawing and offering rational explanations. "Staying in there" and keeping in direct contact with Mary were the hardest things he had to do in his life.
>
> Mary had to overcome the "demon" inside herself in order to see beyond her own hurt and reach out to Dick. Her jealousy and the horrible fear that she would be "used" again were powerful impulses that wanted to inflict more pain on her husband! But as she confronted him with the intent to reestablish something, the miracle did happen and the wall started breaking down.
>
> Their first attempts at breaking through the wall made both of them feel very awkward and stupid! It would have been so easy to call it quits after the first week and to say, "Well, we tried." But both found the strength to win the inner struggle and determined to keep trying—until the wall finally began to crumble. It took a long time for the real breakthrough to shift the awful mood that was between them, but it signaled that the spirit of their relationship had come back. The struggle had been worth it!

And now what about *your marriage!* As is evident in this illustration, you cannot recreate the spirit of your marriage. You cannot wish such a spirit into existence or try to fake its presence. The spirit "goes where it wills" and you do not have control over it! It is not yours to create.

But you can confront the wall that has blocked the flow

of the spirit between the two of you. Let's go back to the analogy of an electric current. When the two of you are in contact (the switch is "on"), the energy can flow unobstructed and your emotions can be in their healthy state of flux. You can experience sadness, happiness, disappointment, hurt, and fulfillment as the circuit of your relationship is open.

A mood is possible between the two of you only when you break contact. The flow of emotion stops and your energy has no place to go. So you pout, hold a grudge, plan revenge, or nurse depression. The flow of the spirit of your relationship is stopped as the emotion gets stuck in one place—in a mood.

All that it takes to get out of such a mood is to come into contact with each other again—*direct contact*, like turning on a switch. You instinctively know that such contact will change your mood! Just watch a child try to pout. He will nurse his mood and will turn away, resisting any contact. But it takes only moments for his mood to change if contact is reestablished with the child. A hug, a smile, or a moment spent to listen can change the mood in a hurry.

The importance of confronting and overcoming the wall between the two of you cannot be overstated, but neither can it's difficulty. Whether or not you will have the continued desire to work on your marriage depends upon reestablishing contact. It is the only way of changing: "We ought to work things out" to *"I want to* work things out." The first has no motivational force to it— no spirit in its statement of duty. The second carries with it the motivation for growth in your marriage. To be able to say that you want to be with your spouse or that you look forward to sharing something with him or her is another way of saying that the spirit of your marriage is back.

The power necessary to effect confrontation has to come from both of you. You must use the strength of your willpower coupled with the emotional power that your determination can give. To activate your willpower, you need to do some honest soul-searching. You must cut away all the excuses, blaming, and defenses—and bring yourself to the basic decision-point. The critical question you need to ask yourself is: "What is more important to me, my marriage relationship or my own selfish needs?"

This is a value-judgment only *you* can make. It needs to be made openly and honestly, otherwise it makes no sense to go through the motions of working on your marriage! Without the willpower that this decision gives, the negative aspects of the initial contact will produce any number of excuses that will sabotage further attempts at restoring the marriage.

When two people seek counseling and one is just going through the motions with no real *intent* to follow through, the lack of willpower quickly shows up. "Well, I guess we can try," or "I was waiting for him (or her) to do something first," or "I was a little too busy this past week," are suspect statements. These are low energy and defensive statements. The willpower is just not there! Have you decided that your marriage relationship is more important than your individual needs? If so, you can make that decision stick.

Let's take another look at Dick and Mary. Their relationship improved after the devastating effects of the affair when they both firmly resolved to work through this feeling. But what was it that really led to the breakthrough? Take a look at one of the sessions:

> Mary still felt her disgust as she looked at Dick, and told him so. Dick started to back down, but then, as he stayed in contact with Mary, he found a new source of strength. He felt a determination to break through her

continued obsession with the affair. His eyes snapped at her as he started talking about the misery he had been through since the affair. He ended up by saying, "I admit that I ruined our relationship by the affair, but can't you try to forgive and let us start over again?"

Mary felt the difference immediately and was startled by the strength in his voice. He was no longer that gutless creature that she could easily reduce to nothing. There was energy there again and she began once more to respect him. She realized that he did care about the relationship enough to put energy into it. She couldn't take his hedging, backing off, and careful explanations. This is what her emotions needed—his directness and his energy!

As Mary's face softened, Dick felt like talking more. He described the torment he had been going through. Mary believed him when he said that he would give anything if the affair had not happened. He then shared his feeling of evasiveness with her. It was like everything draining out of his head when he started feeling trapped. Then there came a panic in his chest that made him feel like a trapped animal that will take any chance to escape. He revealed that it took all the strength he could muster to overcome the panic and stay in contact with her.

Mary understood the depth of that feeling and tears came to her eyes. This was the first time in their relationship that she got a glimpse of his real feelings and it drew her close to him to be able to share his hurt. She forgot about her own demon for awhile and there were minutes of peace between them.

The breakthrough in Dick and Mary's struggle to overcome the demonic effects of his affair came when Mary felt his energy. She knew that he meant business and at that moment a flash of trust came back!

There are three things that can help your determination break through the wall. The first is *expectation*. A contract or a prior agreement can set the stage for confrontation. If both of you have agreed in advance to sit down and talk at a certain time, such an expectation can help break the ice.

The second thing is the added strength that *writing* down your thoughts and feelings gives for your openness and honesty. Face-to-face communication is sometimes impossible when things are very bad between the two of you and a written communication can help your intent "break through." It is easier to be honest in writing down your feelings when you don't have to face the other person's reaction at that moment. When talking directly to each other, the instant feedback that is received can be very inhibiting. You may start to say something important, but then start hedging when you sense disapproval or misunderstanding.

The third thing that is often helpful in creating a better atmosphere for confrontation is the presence of a *third person*. When things are very tense between the two of you, the addition of another person creates a new mix in the situation. Especially if that third person is understanding, open, and a good listener, the mood can shift enough to allow for the situation to be confronted. It required the presence of a counselor for Dick and Mary to be able to confront each other for the first time with the intent to work things out.

These three aids are not really needed if the wall is still freshly-laid and there is just a temporary break in contact between the two of you. This happens in the normal ups and downs of every relationship and contact can be reestablished when the two of you cool down. The problem can be talked through at the next convenient time—because the two of you still want to get back together.

But when the spirit of your marriage has been severely weakened and the wall between you has been allowed to grow, it is no longer natural to reestablish contact.

When the mood is bad enough so that it is hard to find the desire to confront the problems—then your relationship can use some help. At this time it is helpful to 1) set the stage with a contract or agreement to get together at the same time and place each evening to confront your problems; 2) write down your thoughts and feelings beforehand to allow for greater openness; and 3) include a third person initially to help soften the atmosphere.

Now, when you are actually face to face with the wall and have the determination to do something about it, how do you proceed? What steps do you take to break out of the bad mood?

The first step is to establish and maintain *contact* with each other throughout the confrontation session! Remove distracting influences, such as TV or newspaper, and sit so that you are looking at each other.

Eye contact is essential. You might sit and do nothing but look at each other for the first 30 seconds of the session. This can be powerful and is the best way to initiate contact with each other. You cannot completely hide your feelings from your eyes—they remain the "window to your soul." That is why you find yourself not looking at each other when you are upset. Eye contact closes the circuit between the two of you faster than anything else, and forces you to reckon with each other!

Having your voice connected to your thoughts and feelings is also important. To talk without thinking is helpful as the two of you establish verbal communication. Speaking openly, allowing your emotion to be reflected in your voice, enhances contact. The listener is as much tuned in to the emotion reflected in your voice as to the content of what you say. An emotionless conversation just does not ring true—there is no connection between the voice and the feelings.

Then *pay attention* to what is being said. It is easy to

lose contact by letting your mind wander. Not paying attention by thinking of something else is a nice, safe way of keeping yourself from being affected by what is being said. If you are "not there," there can be no real contact.

When you feel the contact slipping, it takes your will-power and determination to stay in there. Whatever mood you are in, determination can break through and force you into action! It puts energy into your head and lets you take over control of your actions. As you feel your eyes shifting down to the floor or as you feel your voice starting to hedge, summoning your determination is like clenching your fists and yelling to yourself, "Stop it! You are going to keep at it until you work it out!" That will bring your energy back into the session.

After good contact has been established, then *set the agenda*. Focus on what is between the two of you. Don't beat around the bush. Bring up the specific situation that is on your mind. Come out directly with it so that the air can be cleared between the two of you. Be willing to say what's on your mind.

When you confront the situation, keep your finger pointed at yourself—rather than immediately accusing your spouse of something. Remember that these are your feelings. Express them as your feelings—the best way the situation affected you rather than accusing the other person.

The following are examples of two ways of confronting a situation:

Finger Pointed at Other Person	**Finger Pointed at Self**
1. Why didn't you support me last night when Beth criticized our children?	1. When Beth criticized our children last night, I got very upset and then felt shaky—I really needed your support then.

2. You're always complaining about something. I can never do anything right.

2. It hurts me to see you upset and I feel helpless when you attack me.

3. What? How much did you pay for that coat? I just can't trust you with money!

3. When you spend money like that, I get an insecure feeling and feel that the finances of the family are all on my shoulders.

4. You only pay attention to me when you want to go to bed.

4. I don't feel very important to you sometimes and then have that awful fear that sex is all you want from me.

5. Boy, you made a fool out of yourself the way you were flirting around all night!

5. It hurts me to see that you enjoy talking to other people more than to me— I felt very unattractive last night when I noticed how much you enjoyed talking to those other people.

Then as you express how the situation made you feel, remember that there is also another side to the story! Each of you helped put the bricks up, but it is always easier to see what the other person has done than accept part of the blame. It is always easier to see the mote in the other person's eye than to be aware of the beam in your own eye! To start out the session by criticizing the other person and recounting all the ways he or she is at fault is the easiest way to destroy any hope that the session will be helpful.

To be open to the possibility that your actions have helped to dampen or kill the spirit of your marriage immediately creates a different atmosphere for the conversation. This goes against everything that is natural, and again it takes your willpower to keep the focus on your spouse. That is just the way you naturally see things—from your own perspective. When you are hurt, it is hard to see, much less to admit your contribution to the breakdown of the relationship.

But, as was stated above, no wall was ever built by one person! Sure, it was his (or her) insensitivity, but it was also your pouting and the way you nursed your hurt feelings that kept the wall in place! And as you look for the way you helped hurt your marriage and have the courage to admit it, you give the confrontation session the chance it desperately needs to open the way for knocking down some of the bricks! It really helps to keep your finger pointed toward yourself while talking.

Then be sure to listen to the other person! It is so easy to prejudge what that person is going to say and to start formulating your rebuttal while he or she is still talking. The art of listening does not come naturally—and again it takes the power of your determination to reach out and do nothing but listen. What your spouse says will definitely arouse emotion in you and you will feel attacked, put down, and eager to contradict.

To listen means to look beyond your own hurt and your needs to see what the other person's world is like. A glimpse of your spouse's hurt is the *understanding* that builds the channel of openness through the wall. The basis of any relationship lies in the feelings that each person gets when they realize that what they shared was understood! There is no other feeling like that one. Feeling understood is a powerful force that will draw you close to that other person. Your listening and understanding means that you have reached through the wall and have touched the other person's world. For that moment, the two of you are one. You are in contact and the spirit of your marriage has a chance for life!

Sometimes it takes days or weeks of confrontation to be able to break through the wall, depending on how thick and high, it has become. If the wall has been allowed to grow for years, it might take many discouraging sessions to finally bore through the thick "mood" between the two of you. Perhaps, the wall has gotten too strong for you to get through—and your attempts will fail. But if there is any hope left for your marriage, direct confrontation with each other to restore contact is the way to work things out.

Confrontation of the wall allows for old wounds to be healed and the unfinished business (finally) to be put to rest. Hurt feelings do not go away until the situation is confronted and worked through. If contact is lost in the middle of something hurtful, those feelings remain to haunt the relationship! Perhaps they seem to disappear, but they have a way of flashing back into your mind to add fuel to other conflicts.

> The best example I can give occurred in Alan and Jill's relationship. He went further than she wanted when they were in the parked car together before they were married, leaving her feeling dirty, cheap, and used. She never shared this with him, but continued to go parking with him, only to reexperience those feelings the next morning. After they were married, she thought sex would then be happy and fulfilling. She found, however, that the thoughts of her being "used" kept flashing in her mind, keeping her from any good feelings on her honeymoon or in the years after that. It was only when she could directly share these hurt feelings with her husband and gain his understanding that she could forgive him and put the past to rest. She was satisfied for the first time in their sexual relationship that same night.

Through such open confrontation, the two of you can also "lay to rest" the things that are between you. When these areas of conflict are opened up and both of you admit your part in building the wall, you can finally forgive each other and open up the flow of energy between you in this area. Forgiveness after honest confrontation always restores the spirit of your relationship.

The following chapter is an extended illustration of a couple who had quite a wall to break through. Their relationship went through as bad a time as anyone I have known. There were times when divorce seemed the best way out. . . .

10 The Spirit Restored

PAUL AND KATHY MET IN HIGH SCHOOL. They had seen each other many times before, but he really didn't notice her until they were in a chemistry class together and were assigned to work on an experiment. He was not too happy to have her as his partner since she didn't seem too smart and he wanted to get a good grade on the project. He came from a very poor background and had to work hard to get where he was—and he did not like to have anyone get in his way. In fact, he quickly got disgusted with anyone who would give up or complain. When he set his mind to something, he got it done.

Kathy had seen Paul around before and for some time had secretly admired him. She felt inadequate around him and when she learned that they were to work together, she was both scared and excited. But then, she had been scared most of her life. This was because her father would always seem to take out his anger on her and would sometimes beat her until she could hardly walk. She grew to fear the time her father would come home.

She still had vivid memories of the day she happened to spill a glass of water when talking to a girlfriend over the phone. Her father was just coming in the door from work—and his face twisted into an ugly snarl as he saw what happened. His eyes seemed a little crazy as he grabbed Kathy and threw her to the floor, yelling at her for being so stupid. She had bruises for weeks where he kicked her.

So the two of them, Paul and Kathy, met in the chemistry lab and found each other. He felt her admiration as he took over the project and she felt his tenderness and patience as she tried to help. They saw each other again that night and many times after that. He would always make the dates and plan the evenings, but Kathy needed his tenderness and affection so much that she did not openly react to his dominance. They both wanted to get together often and usually ended up parked somewhere— not talking much, but enjoying each other's presence.

Paul did feel his anger flare up inside as Kathy would do something to contradict him (just like his father would flare up at his mother), but he would hold back and patiently try to correct her. It was easy to forget those "little" things when she was back in his arms again that evening. He was confident that she would never really contradict him after they were married and let him be the proper head of the house. "After all, that was the way things should be," he heard many times from his father.

Kathy also felt angry and rebellious from time to time when it seemed that Paul was putting her down. She felt her old stubbornness coming back when he would give his commands. Sometimes they would feel too much like her father's demands which she finally had to rebel against to keep her own spirit from getting crushed. But her rebellious feelings soon passed when she saw Paul's concern for her again—especially when he would hold her tightly and stroke her hair.

For the first eight years of their marriage, Paul and Kathy seemed to be content together. Paul devoted much of his energy to his work and succeeded in gaining promotion after promotion—ending up as the production manager. After so many years of struggling and fighting his poverty background, he finally made it! In his fantasies, he was like the "little engine that could." He was the engine, climbing up a long track with his wife and children hooked up behind him. He was the one responsible for getting the whole family on top and he had finally made it up the long hill.

Kathy was also content at first to be married and to feel the security of a husband who cared for her. She felt a good spirit in their relationship even though she soon realized that Paul would not allow her to express her opinion. But then, she had never been able to speak up to her father, so she held in her feelings and tried to make the best of it. She found her own things to do and then was busy enough when the children came.

But as the years went by without Paul and Kathy being able to talk over their feelings, she began to feel strangely unfulfilled. She knew she was a good mother, but felt more and more like a stranger to her husband. He never seemed to feel that she had anything to contribute to his life and if she did offer a suggestion, he would immediately make her feel stupid for having that idea. After eight years, it seemed that she had a consistent feeling of inferiority to Paul.

Paul knew that Kathy had some problems with her feelings of worthlessness, but blamed them on her background and hoped she would grow out of them. He did find himself getting more and more irritated with her as the years went by because it seemed that she was getting lazier. He would criticize her for not having supper ready when he came home. With all of the things that were on his mind, she could at least take care of the "woman's" chores. At times like this, his disgust for her inadequacies would show through in his anger and she would retreat into the bedroom, crying. With a shake of his head, Paul would then fix supper for himself and the children. Kathy would cry herself to sleep at night.

Kathy did try to talk about her frustrations to Paul over the years, but even though Paul seemed to listen, she would come away with the horrible feeling that he really did not understand what she had shared. She had so much trouble expressing herself anyway and when she tried to open up her deeper feelings, he would get impatient with her hesitancy and would try to put words into her mouth. She would then give up after a few minutes and let him think he was right in interpreting her feelings for her. Then, if she did give him a glimpse of her deeper feelings, it would seem like his mind just filed them away like it did everything else. She could not feel that he understood or that he really cared for her as a person.

Paul's job helped amplify his lack of emotional response to Kathy. He was in contact with hundreds of people each week and had to develop ways of dealing with these people. He found out very quickly that being soft did not work. He would never get anywhere if he followed his emotions and reacted to every sob story. When it was good for the company to fire someone, he had to carry through even though he knew that he had a sick wife and 5 children. He couldn't let that bother him or he would become ineffective and be fired himself. He saw too many people who couldn't make it in the tough business world.

So Paul's already tough personality had hardened even more over the eight years and he ended up virtually unable to react to Kathy in a gentle, emotional way. She could no longer see the tenderness and affection that had attracted her to him in the first place. He seemed to her more and more like her father had been. It was so hard to get through to him, so she shared less and less with him. By the end of the eight years, they had gotten into the habit of avoiding each other. They did not even talk over important decisions. He would bring up the matter, but would already have his mind made up and Kathy felt the futility of trying to offer her thoughts.

There was a definite wall between them by the time the two children went off to school. Kathy sat home alone, unable to find the energy to do anything. She felt that her own spirit was crushed—just like when she was a child and was put-down so badly by her father. She was totally frustrated with her life.

As she looked back on their relationship, she shook her head sadly. She could remember how wonderful it was to touch and to hold Paul at the beginning. Now she only felt cold and clammy when he would reach for her in bed. Instead of wanting his touch, she tried to get as far away from him as possible. She developed the habit of staying up long after he went to bed at night to make sure that he was asleep. It turned her off to think that he only wanted to touch her when he needed to use her for his own gratification. For the past several years she had ended up feeling dirty and used after they had sex. There was nothing there for her anymore.

At this critical point in their relationship, Kathy met a friend through their church who also needed someone to talk to. The friend was a woman who had just gone through a divorce and had been struggling with her own feelings. The two of them talked for hours—many times until quite late at night. For the first time, Kathy began sharing her thoughts and feelings with someone.

At first, Kathy felt that what she wanted to say would sound stupid and she had difficulty in expressing her thoughts. But as she found acceptance, she continued opening up, genuinely impressing her friend with the depth of her insight. The conversations continued for over a year and, with the help of a number of books on self-growth, Kathy gradually began to change her image of herself. She no longer felt that she was to blame for everything and realized that she did have a lot to offer to her relationship with Paul. She gradually started resisting her husband's decisions — she started rebelling against his total control of their family.

Paul's first reaction to Kathy's rebellion was to come on even stronger. He found at first that he could still get her to back down and submit to his way of thinking. It angered him that she was making it harder for him to carry out his "responsibilities." He had enough to consider without having his wife buck everything he tried to do. After all, he did have the welfare of the family in mind when he made his decisions.

He was firmly convinced that the husband should be the head of the house and that for him to give in to his wife would not only destroy his masculinity, but would be against God's will. So he came down harder on Kathy and a number of times got so angry that he lost control and hit her. Things were all wrong and it was getting harder and harder for him to want to come home at night. He was almost glad when Kathy would go over to her friend's house. There was too much tension when she was there with him. He also found it harder to get up the desire to reach for her when they were in bed together. It was so hard to be tender to her!

The situation finally reached the critical point. The spirit of their marriage was in deep trouble. The wall of hate between them had grown so high that understanding and tenderness were out of the question. Anything that was said was taken to be a put-down or an act of rebellion. There was no love between them anymore. That is when Kathy finally forced the issue.

Paul had decided to buy a car that he had dreamed about for a long time, thinking that he had worked hard enough for it and deserved this reward. So he went out and bought it, but came home to a very angry wife! Kathy laid into him about failing to take her into consideration. She pointed out that her thriftiness had also helped them save money and *commanded* him to take the car back.

Paul looked at her startled. She had never commanded him to do anything before. He felt a surge of anger and told her that she did not have anything to say about it. She glared right back at him and gave him an ultimatum —"Either the car goes, or you go!" She meant it and the fire in her eyes hit home. There would be no more submission to Paul's decrees.

They argued for a long time, yelling and threatening each other. Paul got so angry that he hit Kathy hard enough to knock her down. Her eyes were as cold as steel when she got back and pushed him against the wall. With her face just inches from his, she screamed, "Get out of here. I hate you!"

He left the house and drove for a long time. It seemed like a nightmare that he had lost his home, and he pored over his situation again and again. As he thought of divorce, he realized what a loss that would be to him. All of his married life, he struggled to make a good living for his family—but what good was an engine struggling up the track if there was nothing behind to pull? In a moment of deep emotion, he realized how much he needed his family. He found himself willing to try to regain the spirit of their marriage.

Kathy refused when he suggested that they seek help, because she was afraid he was just trying to get her back into her place. But when he showed that he was genuinely interested in doing something about their relationship by letting her choose someone to go to, she agreed to it. She had very little hope that Paul could ever change —and she was not going through the next decade of her life being put down all the time.

When they first came into my office, Paul did all the talking. He was obviously embarrassed to admit to marital problems and started off trying to minimize the difficulty. One piercing glance from his wife, however, forced him to admit that they were close to divorce. He then went on to point out how Kathy had changed over the past year and as a result of her kick on self-worth had ruined what he thought was a pretty good marriage. For about twenty minutes all his remarks seemed to say, "If only she hadn't changed."

Kathy would not let his accusations go without pointing out his neglect of her over the years. She told of her feelings of worthlessness and how he managed to keep putting her down by his harshness to her. They were close to a fight again and Kathy felt a hopelessness creep over her.

The presence of a third person, however, caused a different atmosphere than the one that was usually present when the two of them were alone. There was a safety in having another person between them. Even though I did little but listen, both Paul and Kathy felt understood. There was less need to push their point home and keep hammering away at it like they did when they were alone. After both had presented their side, they lapsed into silence.

Paul and Kathy had been ignoring each other all this time. They did not look at each other, except in quick glances, and really did not do much to contact each other. In fact, that was the way they were when they argued—they wouldn't look at each other and would not really listen to each other. The wall between them that kept them out of contact was quite evident in the office.

I then asked them to do only two things: 1) to look directly at each other and listen to each other without interruption as they talked and 2) to see if each could take half the blame for the problems and admit or confess those things to the other.

Neither Paul nor Kathy wanted to follow those instructions! They did not want to look directly at each other and certainly they did not want to give the other an advantage by admitting some faults! They just about stopped at this point.

But then Paul found the strength of will to try. He pulled his chair around to face Kathy and their eyes searched each other for the first time since either of them could remember. They sat in silence for a few moments, confronting each other. Almost immediately Kathy felt the attempt in his eyes to stare her down and found her eyes growing hard and rebellious. The ways he had hurt her flashed back into her mind and she just wanted to let him know that he could not put her down anymore. She was now someone he would have to reckon with.

Paul did not like the thought of contact from the beginning and when he first looked at Kathy, he felt very defensive. He was inwardly shaken by the directness of the contact. He thought her expression too hard and steeled himself for the rebellion he knew was coming.

The first twenty seconds seemed like a stare-down and neither wanted to break the silence. But with my urging, each tried to look beyond the "wall" and see the other person as they were. Paul immediately found himself afraid, much to his surprise, and quickly looked away to regain control. Kathy picked up the change in Paul immediately and felt her eyes grow softer. At that moment she saw his struggle. Her eyes started to cloud up as she realized the pain he was going through and then, for a split second, she actually wanted to reach out for him! Paul, in turn, felt the change in Kathy's eyes and was puzzled—he had expected the hardness to continue. He didn't trust it yet, but it felt like there was a tiny hole in the wall and that something good passed between them at that moment.

The spell was broken as Paul began to talk. Kathy felt herself stiffen and look away as he brought up the subject of her rebellion toward him. Paul was honestly going to say something about his neglect of her, but he did not get that far before Kathy stopped listening and planned her rebuttal for the put-down she felt coming.

They walked out of the office feeling angry with each other again—with little hope to break through to each other.

That night, at Paul's insistence, they sat down after the children were in bed and tried to talk to each other again. It was very difficult and painful for both of them, but they forced themselves to come into contact again and tried to listen to each other. They were anxious and felt awkward looking at each other, so Paul started asking Kathy questions. She tried to open up to him, but felt him pressuring her and could not continue. She just wanted to get out of there! But she stayed and tried again to look at him. It just did not feel right!

Paul tried to talk also and Kathy struggled to listen

and not react to what he was saying. But he seemed to bring up the subjects that would lead to her problems and Kathy felt him point the finger at her again. She started resisting him and the session ended up in the usual argument. They went to bed angry at each other and ready to call it quits.

The next night they somehow found the strength to try it again and sat down facing each other. The wall seemed even higher as they looked at each other. It was so evident that there was little love between them and neither really wanted to start talking. But as they stayed in contact, Paul had a flash of the good times they had when they were dating each other and realized how worn and unhappy Kathy was now. He felt sorry for her—and the hole appeared in the wall again. They both felt a flash of concern pass between them before the hole closed up again and they went back to their guardedness.

Nothing else came of that second evening and the third evening neither wanted to try to talk because of the evident tension in the house. The mood was too nasty to try to break through it. The following evening was a Friday and Paul, after doing some heavy thinking at the office, asked Kathy to go out to eat. She was surprised and suspicious—they had not been out together for such a long time. The mood was still tense between them as they ate, but not nearly as bad as it had been the night before. They did not say much until they settled back to some coffee after the meal. They had looked at each other several times during the meal, but there seemed to be no breaks in the wall between them and both were left feeling nothing toward each other.

Paul had rehearsed something and tried to choose his words carefully as he started talking. He said that he had done a lot of thinking and had begun to recognize the ways that he had been hurtful. He then continued, "This might come as a surprise to you, but the main reason I did not listen to you was so that I would not have to re-think my decisions. I knew that you would have some valid thoughts to offer and then I would have to spend all that time taking them into consideration. There were so many things on my mind that it was easier to cut you off."

Paul said these words in a guarded tone without much emotion and watched Kathy carefully for her reaction. He expected her to begin an argument. But Kathy sat up in surprise! It was the first time he ever suggested that what she had to say was worthwhile. She was stunned as she sat in silence, her mind going a mile a minute. His words made her feel a spark of hope inside, but immediately she suspected that he was just saying that to appease her.

Paul saw the surprise in her and again felt a break in the wall as that good feeling passed between them. He blew it, however, as he went on to point out that there were certain areas that he knew best and should make the decisions. But the spark had been there for a moment and both had experienced it. That was enough to get them to try again.

It was almost a week after that—a week of struggle for both of them to try to talk to each other—that a real breakthrough came in their relationship. They were discussing possible divorce again and Paul found the strength to say that he wanted his family more than he wanted anything else in life. He said that the reason he was willing to struggle through their crumbling relation-ship was that he felt an emptiness when he thought of losing the family.

Again, Kathy sat up in surprise. She had been looking at him while he was talking and could see the moistness in his eyes as he said those words. Suddenly she found that she believed him! As her eyes softened, a strong feeling passed between them. It was as though the bricks were beginning to fall from the wall.

Kathy was then able to share her feelings of unimportance. She recalled the many times she had retreated to her room in tears because she felt so inadequate. It was almost as if a dam had broken and her pent-up feelings came rushing out. She said a lot in those few minutes and some of the things left Paul sitting on the edge of his seat, wanting to contradict her.

She kept talking and finally, in tears, came to her deepest feeling—she just wanted to be someone of importance in her husband's eyes. She just wanted to be treated like a person by him—and for the first time *Paul could see past her rebellion.* He caught a glimpse of her need, and a light dawned on him! His eyes were softer than she had seen them for years, and without thinking, he was moved to reach out and touch her hand. She felt his concern and broke down crying—and they shared a powerful moment together! Something was alive between them again.

It took them three evenings to get that feeling back again. Kathy started out by talking about her fear of being crushed—a threatened feeling. Paul immediately started questioning that feeling, implying that it was foolish to have that fear and Kathy felt like stopping. She snapped at him, "Why don't you ever listen?" Paul felt his own anger flare up, but something made him stop and think about what had happened. He realized that he did not try to understand Kathy's feelings, but always felt the pressure to "do something" about them. He shared this insight with Kathy and she felt her mood change enough to continue. She could describe her feeling as a steamroller that was heading toward her. She either had to run or defend herself from it.

Paul got the picture and looked at Kathy questioningly. He knew all about her background, but had never stopped to realize how powerful the feelings related to her father's authority were inside her. "No wonder she naturally took everything I said as an attempt to crush her," he thought. He suddenly wanted to hear more. Kathy felt this urge of interest and was warmed by it. She opened up more and as she described the powerlessness and confusion she felt when it seemed that she had lost again, she felt a real spark of understanding from Paul.

There was something in his eyes she had not seen there for years. His understanding melted her and she started pouring out her feelings. For a few hours, it was just like when they were first married! They felt close and peaceful with each other and finally fell asleep touching each other. The spirit of their marriage was back—a miracle had happened that night!

But Paul woke up again the next morning feeling guarded and came across to Kathy as being preoccupied again. He seemed to act as if the previous evening had not happened. Kathy felt betrayed and her anger built up over his lack of response. She finally blew up at him as he left for work and the wall was back to normal. They didn't tell each other "good-bye" and did not feel like looking at each other when he returned home that evening.

They did not talk for several nights after that—but then they tried it again. Kathy immediately demanded that Paul tell her why he had been so cold to her after she felt so close to him that night. Paul did not feel like giving in to the demand, but swallowed and admitted that he had been genuinely moved that evening, but was afraid it would not last and woke up feeling foolish for letting Kathy affect him so much. He was afraid she could really dominate him if he let his emotions go like that.

Kathy felt a glimmer of understanding—as if she was actually seeing Paul's emotional structure as he talked—and urged Paul to continue. He just shrugged his shoulders and said that there was no more to be said. Kathy realized at that moment that it was very hard for Paul to admit his feelings and she tried to show him that she understood. Something got through and before the evening was over, Paul revealed some of his fears to her. He had the image of weakness associated with expressing feelings and realized how much he tried to block out what he felt.

They felt very close again that night and were able to continue the mood over to the next evening. They were able to talk about their sexual feelings toward each other and it was 3:00 A.M. before either of them realized the time! They were both surprised at what they found out. When Kathy expressed the strength of her sexual desires and her wish for Paul to be gentle in arousing her, Paul was stunned. He had resigned himself to her frigidity, but now felt a new hope.

Paul, in turn, shared his feelings of anxiety in his sexual attempts and Kathy understood. For the first time ever in their relationship, Paul was able to show his consideration of Kathy with his tenderness as they were in bed. They also talked to each other as they made *love* for the first time ever and both went to sleep satisfied.

There were yet to be many periods of anger and rebellion for Paul and Kathy and a number of times they lost contact with each other. But as they confronted each other and brought up the things that had built up the wall in the first place, the bricks seemed to start loosening up and the energy started flowing more freely between the two of them. More and more often the spark reappeared between them. At the end of three months, Kathy was moved to write the following:

I am happy to say that things are going very well between the two of us. I wanted to tell you that we are making it and it seems to be getting easier. We both hoped that we could find a way of staying together, but we never imagined we would end up really *wanting* to be together!

It's still hard to believe that we have come from having no relationship at all to developing a very good one.

11 A Goal for Your Marriage

WHAT DO YOU THINK ABOUT YOUR MARRIAGE NOW? Are you beginning to understand that your relationship needs daily attention for it to grow? Do you see that the spirit between the two of you can get blocked and will be seriously weakened if the wall is allowed to remain over a period of time? Do you have some idea of how to restore contact and break through the bad moods? Do you know what it takes to develop clear understanding and communication?

Now you need to put all of this to work. Perhaps it would be helpful to introduce an example of what can happen in your marriage so that you can more clearly see what it is you need to devote your energy toward.

In casting about for such an example, I happened to notice my son's hands. He plays outside almost every day in the red clay soil of the Piedmont area of North Carolina. Before supper *every day* he has to take a few minutes to scrub his hands with the direct contact of hot, soapy water. If he misses an evening, the next day his

hands are harder to get clean because the reddish color
has gotten into his skin. Then he needs to scrub even
harder. Likewise, you can consider the daily buildup of
"dirt" in your relationship that needs to be confronted
and "washed away" by good contact. If the "dirt" is just
smoothed over or covered up, it becomes harder and
harder to wash out.

So where do you put your energy? Definitely *not* in
trying to smooth things over—*not* in covering up whatever things that might come between you, but you must
put your energy into *remaining in contact.* Trust in the
spirit to be able to handle any honest feelings or reactions. Confront each other with the intention of working
things out. Keep the channel clear. Knock down the wall.
Keep the relationship current. Don't let unfinished business pile up. Continually reestablish contact with each
other.

When things are going well—when there is a good
spirit in your marriage, use this positive motivation to
establish good habits of sharing and opening up to each
other. This is a time to practice getting into each other's
world—to practice good listening skills. This is also a
time to learn how to share your feelings. This is a time
to practice opening up to each other to give a clearer
picture of the significance of different events. This is a
time to grow in your understanding and closeness to
each other. Value this time and take advantage of it.

But when things are tense, struggle to restore contact.
Above all, *do not let a bad mood continue.* Swallow your
pride and put all of your energy into confronting the wall
that has come between the two of you. Sit down and
work things out! This is a critical time when you need
to go against your natural impulse to avoid each other.
Break the mood as soon as you can.

That brings me to a good measuring device for the spirit of your marriage. If you take the degree to which your marriage stays smooth as evidence of a good spirit, you're using the wrong yardstick. That would not necessarily mean that there is much energy present. You could just be covering things up and letting things build underneath.

Rather, the best way to assess the health of your marriage is by the speed with which things can be worked out. If moods or bad feelings stay around for days, watch out! The spirit of your marriage is in danger. If, however, the moods are broken fairly quickly and your emotions don't get stuck in one spot, but are allowed to move on, then the spirit is free to be expressed.

In a Christian sense, this is called the freedom of the Gospel. Living under the Gospel is a healthy recognition that you *will* sin against each other. Such admission keeps you from putting your energy into the wrong place. It frees you from having to watch everything you do, lest it be sinful. It frees you to put your energy into something far more productive—it frees you to struggle against the wall. Your energy can then be directed toward confrontation and restoring contact—toward reconciliation.

Living under the Gospel is to put confession and forgiveness at the top of your priority list. This is the means by which you get back into contact with each other and restore the spirit of your marriage. Confession is the way to soften up the wall. This action points the finger at self and immediately takes the pressure off the wall. Instead of the usual accusations, blaming, and hard feelings, you now soften up the wall by recognizing and taking responsibility for the bricks you help put up. Confession or pointing the finger at self opens up the way for breaking down the tense mood. This can stop the vicious cycle of defending self and putting the blame on the other person

—who in turn then must defend self and find ways of getting back.

Such confession does not mean playing the part of a martyr. It does not mean agreeing to something just to smooth things over. It does not mean admitting something in order to get your spouse to admit his (or her) part. Confession is the painful process of "dying to sin" (Rom. 6:11). It is the inner struggle to see the beam in your own eye rather than letting the focus be upon the mote in your spouse's eye (Matt. 7:3). Confession is the painful, honest admission of your own pettiness, selfishness, and smallness. It forces out into the open your favorite ways of sinning. It takes the facade of goodness away and exposes the "dirt" of your character. It is the ultimate of personal honesty.

After confession has paved the way, then forgiveness becomes the power that breaks down the wall. As the wall is confronted in the presence of each other and you both deeply acknowledge how your sin has helped put the wall in place, then forgiveness can put the matter to rest for good. Only then will you no longer feel the compulsion to get even or to continue to hold a grudge. The spirit of your marriage is free once again to flow between the two of you. Through confession and forgiveness, you are free to find excitement in each other again!

It is at the point of the recreation of the spirit of your marriage that a miracle occurs. This is not something the two of you can do on your own. You are not the ones who do the creating—you can only confront with hope and trust. It takes the Holy Spirit to "renew a right spirit" within your marriage (see Ps. 51:10).

Now just what does the Holy Spirit have to do with your marriage? Well, you might not recognize the reality of his presence. We live in an age that has tried to explain away the spiritual, reducing such "God talk" to the level of polite tolerance within religious language. Thus any real presence of God's hand at work among us is difficult to imagine. This actually then becomes the final blow that our culture delivers to your marriage—to rob it of the power of God's presence.

It is difficult to see the work of the Holy Spirit in your marriage when there seems to be a natural explanation for everything. It is so easy to overlook this reality with eyes that have been trained to focus on the facts and objects of our technological age.

But your marriage relationship is not a *thing*. It is not an object that can be manipulated by a computer or created out of a test tube. There is no synthetic substitute for the presence of love and tenderness. The flow of energy that you can feel between each other cannot be manufactured and marketed.

In similar fashion, you cannot make yourself *want to* be together with your spouse. You can force yourself to come home, but you cannot make yourself *want* to come home. Your spirit and the spirit of your marriage are not under your control. You can pretend that you are enjoying an evening together, but both of you know the truth. You cannot fake the spirit of your marriage.

It is only the creator of all life, who created your marriage relationship in the first place, who can recreate this spirit again. He can recreate any relationship, no matter how high the wall has become—such is his power and the power of forgiveness!

One of the most priceless gifts God has given you is the spirit of your marriage. Value its presence highly. Rejoice when the spirit is good. Struggle to keep in daily contact, keeping yourselves open to each other.

And may the Holy Spirit continue to bless your marriage with his presence. May the spirit of your marriage deepen as you stay in contact with each other.